BEETHOVEN

BEETHOVEN
AT THE AGE OF 21.

(From a Miniature by Gerhard von Kügelgen.)

Frontispiece.]

BEETHOVEN

BY

ROMAIN ROLLAND

TRANSLATED BY

B. CONSTANCE HULL

WITH A BRIEF ANALYSIS OF THE SONATAS, THE
SYMPHONIES, AND THE QUARTETS BY

A. EAGLEFIELD HULL

WITH 24 MUSICAL ILLUSTRATIONS AND 4 PLATES
and an Introduction by EDWARD CARPENTER

THIRD EDITION (Revised)

Select Bibliographies Reprint Series

 BOOKS FOR LIBRARIES PRESS
FREEPORT, NEW YORK

Third Edition First Published 1919
Reprinted 1969

STANDARD BOOK NUMBER:
8369-5077-1

LIBRARY OF CONGRESS CATALOG CARD NUMBER:
76-95077

PRINTED IN THE UNITED STATES OF AMERICA

PREFACE

" I want to prove that whoever acts rightly and nobly, can by that alone bear misfortune "
BEETHOVEN
(To the Municipality of Vienna, Feb. 1, 1819.)

THE air is heavy around us. The world is stifled by a thick and vitiated atmosphere—an undignified materialism which weighs on the mind and heart hindering the work of governments and individuals alike. We are being suffocated. Let us throw open the windows that God's free air may come in, and that we may breathe the breath of heroes.

Life is stern. It is a daily battle for those not content with an unattractive mediocrity of soul. And a sad battle it is, too, for many—a combat without grandeur, without happiness, fought in solitude and silence. Weighed down by poverty and domestic cares, by excessive and senseless tasks which waste the strength to no purpose, without a gleam of hope, many souls are separated from each other, without even the con-

v

solation of holding out a hand to their brothers
in misfortune who ignore them and are ignored
by them. They are forced to rely on themselves
alone; and there are moments when even the
strongest give way under their burden of trouble.
They call out—for a friend.

Let them then gather around themselves the
heroic friends of the past—the great souls who
suffered for the good of universal humanity. The
lives of great men are not written for the proud
or for the ambitious; they are dedicated rather
to the unhappy. And who really is not? To
those who suffer, we offer the balm of their sacred
sufferings. No one is alone in the fight. The
darkness of the world is made clear by the guiding
light of the souls of the heroes.

I do not give the name hero to those who have
triumphed by infinite thought or by sheer physical
strength—but only to those made great by
goodness of heart. Beethoven wrote, " I recognise no sign of superiority in mankind other
than goodness." Where the character is not
great, there is no great man, there is not even a
great artist, nor a great man of action; there are
only idols unearthed for the cheap and short-lived
applause of the multitude; time will efface them
altogether. Outward success matters little. The
only thing is to be great, not to appear so.

The lives of the great heroes were lives of one long martyrdom ; a tragic destiny willed their souls to be forged on the anvil of physical and moral grief, of misery and ill-health. They were made great through their misfortune. Because these mighty souls complained little of their unhappiness, the best of humanity is with them. Let us gather courage from them; for torrents of quiet strength and inspiring goodness issued from their great hearts. Without even consulting their works or hearing their voices, we read in their eyes the secret of their lives—that it is good to have been in trouble, for thence the character acquires even more greatness, happiness and fruition.

. . . . . .

The strong and pure Beethoven himself hoped in the midst of his sufferings that his example would give help to other unfortunate ones. . . . . " that the unhappy being may be consoled in finding another as unfortunate as himself, who in face of all obstacles has done everything possible to become worthy of the name, MAN." After years of battling with almost superhuman efforts to rise superior to his sufferings and accomplish his life's work—to breathe a little more courage into poor weak humanity, this conquering Prometheus ob-

served to a friend who called too much on God,
" O man, help thyself ! "

May we be inspired by his noble words. Animated by the example of this man's faith in life
and his quiet confidence in himself, let us again
take heart.

ROMAIN ROLLAND.

INTRODUCTION

By EDWARD CARPENTER

IT is not very generally recognised that Beethoven
was not only a great musician, but a great leader
and teacher. He freed the human spirit from in-
numerable petty bonds and conventions, he recorded the profoundest experiences of life, and
gave form and utterance to emotions hardly guessed
—certainly not definitely expressed—before his
time. Personally I feel I owe much more to
Beethoven in these respects than I do to Shakespeare: and though this, of course, may be a purely personal or accidental matter, yet I mention it
in order to show that the music of such a man has,
after all, the closest bearing on actual life.

M. Romain Rolland in his excellent little study
has brought this prophetic and inspiring quality
of Beethoven's life and music out very strongly.
He has traced the tragedy of Beethoven's life and
experience, and its culmination in a kind of libera-
tion of his spirit from the bonds of mortality; he

A

has shown how this connects up with the composer's strong sentiment of democracy and sympathy with the suffering masses; and how it leads to the utterance of that strange sense of joy which penetrates and suffuses his later work. In all these respects M. Rolland regards Beethoven as one of the greatest benefactors of humanity.

On the other hand our author builds in the picture of Beethoven's life and character with a great number of small touches derived from all sorts of writers and biographers—and so succeeds in giving a life-like impression of his personality.

EDWARD CARPENTER.

As bearing on the subject of M. Romain Rolland's book, Mr. Carpenter has kindly given permission to insert the following few extracts from his own book, "Angels' Wings."

"Everything conspired in Beethoven to make his utterance authentic, strong, unqualified—like a gushing spring which leaps from the inaccessible depths of the mountain. His solitary habits kept his mind clear from the mud and sediment which the market-place and the forum mistake for thought; his deafness coming on at so early an age (twenty-eight), increased this effect, it left him fancy-free in the world of music; Wagner even mentions the excessive thickness of his skull (ascertained long after his death), as suggesting the special isolation of his brain. From a boy Beethoven was a great reader. He fed his mind in his own way. Unlike the musicians who went before him, he could brook no dependence upon condescending nobilities. He was not going to be a Court fool The man who could rush into the courtyard of his really sincere friend and ' patron,' Prince Lobkowitz, and shout ' Lobkowitz donkey, Lobkowitz donkey,' for all the valets and chamber-maids to hear; or who could leave his humble lodgings because the over-polite landlord of the house would insist on doffing his hat each time they passed on the stairs; must have had ' something of the devil in him!' (This was the verdict of Hummel, Vogler, Gelinck, and others when they first heard him improvise on his arrival at Vienna). In politics, in a quite general way, he evolved radicalism or republicanism as his creed; in religion, though nominally a Catholic, he was quite informal. A pantheist one might perhaps call him, or a mystic after Eckhardt and Tauler. Finally, one may mention, as an indication of the great range and strength of his personality, its exceedingly slow growth. While Mozart at the age of twenty-three had written a great number of Operas, Symphonies, Cantatas and Masses—many of them of quite mature character—Beethoven at the same age had little or nothing to show. His first Symphony and his Septett, which he always looked back upon as childish productions, were not written till about the age of twenty-seven; and his first great Symphony (the *Eroica*) not till he was thirty-two."—*Angels' Wings*, pp. 141-2.

" Beethoven came at the culmination of a long line of musical tradition. He also came at a moment when the foundations of society were breaking away for the preparation of something new. His great strength lay in the fact that he united the old and the new. He was epic and dramatic, and held firmly to the accepted outlines and broad evolution of his art, like the musicians who went before him; he was lyrical, like those who followed, and uttered to the full his own vast individuality. And so (like the greatest artists) he transformed rather than shattered the traditions into which he was born.

" Beethoven was always trying to express *himself;* yet not, be it said, so much any little phase of himself or of his feelings, as the total of his life-experience. He was always trying to reach down and get the fullest, deepest utterance of which his subject in hand was capable, and to relate it to the rest of his experience. But being such as he was, and a master-spirit of his age, when he reached into himself for his own expression, he reached to

the expression also of others—to the expression of
all the thoughts and feelings of that wonderful revolutionary time, seething with the legacy of the
past and germinal with the hopes and aspirations
of the future. Music came to him rich already
with gathered voices; but he enlarged its language
beyond all precedent for the needs of a new humanity."—*Ibid*, pp. 146-7.

"Bettina Brentano, writing to Gœthe of Beethoven, says : ' I am, indeed, only a child, but I am
not on that account wrong in saying (what perhaps
no one yet perceives and believes) that he far sur-
passes the measure of other men. Shall we ever
attain to him ? I doubt it. May he but live till
the lofty problem of his spirit be fully solved; let
him but reach his highest aim, and he will put
into our hands the key to a glorious knowledge
which shall bring us a stage nearer to true blessed-
ness. . . He said himself, "I have no friend,
I must live alone; but I know that in my heart
God is nearer to me than to others. I approach
him without fear, I have always known him.
Neither am I anxious about my music, which no
adverse fate can overtake, and which *will free him
who understands it from the misery which afflicts
others.*"'

"These are wonderful words which are put into
Beethoven's mouth. Though their authenticity

has been doubted, it is difficult, almost impossible, to suppose that the ' child ' or any one else invented them.   On the other hand, they agree strangely with those authentic words of his already quoted, ' Every day I come nearer to the object which I can feel though I cannot describe it.'

" Beethoven is the prophet of the new era which the nineteenth century ushers in for mankind.   As things must be *felt* before they can be acted out; so they may be expressed in the indefinite emotional forms of music, before they can be uttered and definitely imaged forth in words or pictorial shapes.   Beethoven is the forerunner of Shelley and Whitman among the poets, of J. W. Turner and J. F. Millet among the painters.   He is the great poet who holds Nature by the one hand and Man by the other.   Within that low-statured, rudely-outlined figure which a century ago walked hatless through the fields near Mödling or sat oblivious in some shabby restaurant at Vienna, dwelt an emotional giant—a being who—though his outer life by deafness, disease, business-worries, poverty, was shattered as it were into a thousand squalid fragments—in his great heart embraced all mankind, with piercing insight penetrated intellectually through all falsehoods to the truth, and already in his art-work gave outline to the religious, the human, the democratic yearnings, the loves, the comradeship, the daring individualities, and all the heights and depths of feeling of a new dawning era of society. He was in fact, and he gave utterance to, a new type of Man. What that struggle must have been between his inner and outer conditions—of his real self with the lonely and mean surroundings in which it was embodied —we only know through his music. When we listen to it we can understand the world-old tradition that now and then a divine creature from far heavens takes mortal form and suffers in order that it may embrace and redeem mankind."—*Ibid*, pp. 205-7.

CONTENTS

xvii

xviii CONTENTS

LIST OF ILLUSTRATIONS

BEETHOVEN

Woltuen, wo man kann
Freiheit über alles lieben,
Wahrheit nie, auch sogar am
Throne nicht verleugnen.
Beethoven
(Album-leaf, 1792)

To do all the good one can,
To love liberty above everything,
And even if it be for a kingdom,
Never to betray truth.

HIS LIFE

HE was short and thick set, broad shouldered and of athletic build. A big face, ruddy in complexion —except towards the end of his life, when his colour became sickly and yellow, especially in the winter after he had been remaining indoors far from the fields. He had a massive and rugged forehead, extremely black and extraordinarily thick hair through which it seemed the comb had never passed, for it was always very rumpled, veritable bristling " serpents of Medusa."[1] His eyes shone

---

1 J. Russell (1822). Charles Czerny who, when a child, saw him in 1801 with a beard of several days' growth, hair bristling, wearing a waistcoat and trousers of goats' wool, thought he had met Robinson Crusoe.

B

with prodigious force.   It was one of the chief
things one noticed on first encountering him, but
many were mistaken in their colour.   When they
shone out in dark splendour from a sad and tragic
visage, they generally appeared black; but they
were really a bluish grey.[1] Small and very deep-
set, they flashed fiercely in moments of passion or
warmth, and dilated in a peculiar way under the
influence of inspiration, reflecting his thoughts with
a marvellous exactness.[2]   Often they inclined up-
wards with a melancholy expression.   His nose
was short and broad with the nostrils of a lion; the
mouth refined, with the lower lip somewhat promi-
nent.   He had very strong jaws, which would
easily break nuts, a large indentation in his chin
imparted a curious irregularity to the face.   " He
had a charming smile," said Moscheles, " and in
conversation a manner often lovable and inviting
confidence; on the other hand his laugh was most
disagreeable, loud, discordant and strident "—the
laugh of a man unused to happiness.   His usual
expression was one of melancholy.   Rellstab in
1825 said that he had to summon up all his courage
to prevent himself from breaking into tears when
he looked into Beethoven's " tender eyes with their
speaking sadness."   Braun von Braunthal met
him in an inn a year later.   Beethoven was sitting

1 The painter Kloeber's remark, when he painted his portrait
about 1818.
2 Dr. W. C. Müller observed particularly " his fine eloquent
eyes sometimes so kind and tender, at other times so wild,
threatening and awe inspiring " (1820).

in a corner with closed eyes, smoking a long pipe
—a habit which grew on him more and more as he
approached death. A friend spoke to him. He
smiled sadly, drew from his pocket a little note-
tablet, and in a thin voice which frequently
sounded cracked notes, asked him to write down
his request. His face would frequently become
suddenly transfigured, maybe in the access of
sudden inspiration which seized him at random,
even in the street, filling the passers-by with
amazement, or it might be when great thoughts
came to him suddenly, when seated at the piano.
" The muscles of his face would stand out, his
veins would swell; his wild eyes would become
doubly terrible. His lips .trembled, he had the
manner of a wizard controlling the demons which
he had invoked." " . . . . . A Shakespearean
visage—' King Lear¹ ' "—so Sir Julius Benedict
described it.

* * * * * *

LUDWIG VAN BEETHOVEN was born on December 16th, 1770, in a little bare attic of a humble
dwelling at Bonn, a small University town on the
Rhine near Cologne. He came of Flemish

---

1 Kloeber said " Ossian's." All these details are taken from
notes of Beethoven's friends, or from travellers who saw him,
such as Czerny, Moscheles, Kloeber, Daniel Amadeus Atterbohm,
W. C. Müller, J. Russell, Julius Benedict, Rochlitz, etc.

origin.[1] His father was an illiterate and lazy tenor singer—a " good-for-nothing fellow " and a confirmed drunkard. His mother was the daughter of a cook. She had been a maidservant and by her first marriage was the widow of a *valet de chambre*.

Unlike the more fortunate Mozart, Beethoven spent an unhappy childhood devoid of domestic comfort. From his earliest years life was for him a sad, even a brutal, fight for existence. His father wished to exploit the boy's musical talents and to turn him to lucrative purposes as a prodigy. At the age of four he compelled the boy to practise on the harpsichord for hours together and he shut him up alone with the violin, forcing him to work in this way. It is astonishing that the boy was not completely disgusted with music, for the father persisted in this treatment for many years, often resorting to actual violence. Beethoven's youth was saddened by the care and anxiety of earning his daily bread by tasks far too burdensome for his age. When he was eleven years old he was placed in the theatre orchestra; at thirteen he became an organist of the chapel. In 1787 he lost his mother whom he adored. " She was so

1 His grandfather, Ludwig, the most remarkable man of the family and whom Beethoven most resembled, was born at Antwerp, and only settled at Bonn in his twentieth year when he became choir master to the Prince Elector. We must not forget this fact to understand properly the passionate independence of Beethoven's nature and so many other traits which are not really German in his character.

good to me,. so worthy of love, the best friend I had! How happy was I when I could utter that dear name of mother and she could hear it!"[1] She died of consumption and Beethoven believed himself to be affected with the same complaint. Already he suffered continually, and a depression of spirits even more terrible than the physical pain hung over him always.[2] When he was seventeen he was practically the head of the family and responsible for the education of his two younger brothers. He suffered the humiliation of being obliged to beg for a pension for his father, that his father's pension should be paid to himself, as the father only squandered it in drink. These sad experiences made a profound impression on the youth. However, he found great affection and sympathy from a family in Bonn who always remained very dear to him—the Breuning family. The gentle "Lorchen," Eleonore von Breuning, was two years younger than Beethoven. He taught her music and she initiated him into the charms of poetry. She was the companion of his youth and there may have been between them a still more tender sentiment. Later on Eleonore married Dr. Wegeler, one of Beethoven's best friends; and up to Beethoven's last day there existed between the three a deep, steady friendship, amply proven by the regular and loving epistles of

1 Letter to Dr. Schade at Augsburg, 15th September, 1787.
2 Later on, in 1816, he said: " He is a poor man who does not know how to die! I myself knew, when I was but fifteen."

Wegeler and Eleonore, and those of their old faithful friend (*alter treuer Freund*) to the dear good Wegeler (*guter lieber Wegeler*). These friendly bonds became all the more touching as old age crept on all three, and still their hearts remained warm.[1] Beethoven also found a safe guide and good friend in Christian Gottlob Neefe, his music master, whose high moral character had no less influence on the young musician than did his broad and his intelligent, artistic views.

Sad as was the childhood of Beethoven, he always treasured a tender and melancholy memory of the places where it was spent. Though compelled to leave Bonn, and destined to spend nearly the whole of his life in the frivolous city of Vienna with its dull environs, he never forgot the beautiful Rhine valley and the majestic river. " *Unser Vater Rhine* " (our father Rhine) as he called it, was to him almost human in its sympathy, being like some gigantic soul whose deep thoughts are beyond all human reckoning. No part is more beautiful, more powerful, more calm, than that part where the river caresses the shady and flowered slopes of the old University city of Bonn. There Beethoven spent the first twenty years of his life. There the dreams of his waking heart were born—in the fields, which slope languishingly down to the water side, with their

---

1 We quote from several of these letters in a later part of the book, pages 65, *et seq*.

mist-capped poplars, their bushes and their willows and the fruit trees whose roots are steeped in the rapid silent stream. And all along lying gently on the banks, strangely soft, are towns, churches, and even cemeteries, whilst away on the horizon the blue tints of the Seven Mountains show in wild jagged edges against the sky, forming a striking background to the graceful, slender, dream-like silhouettes of old ruined castles. His heart remained ever faithful to the beautiful, natural surroundings of his childhood, and until his very last moment he dreamt of seeing these scenes once again. " My native land, the beautiful country where I first saw the light of day ; it is always as clear and as beautiful in my eyes as when I left it."[1] He never saw it again.

• • • • • •

In November, 1792, Beethoven removed to Vienna, the musical metropolis of Germany.[2] The Revolution had broken out. It threatened to spread over the whole of Europe. Beethoven left Bonn just at the moment when the war

1 To Wegeler, 29th June, 1801.
2 He had already made a short stay there, in the spring of 1787. On that occasion he met Mozart who, however, took little notice of him. Haydn, whose acquaintance he made at Bonn in December, 1790, gave him some lessons. Beethoven also had for masters, Albrechtsberger and Salieri. The first-named taught him Counterpoint and Fugue, the second trained him in vocal writing.

reached it. On his way to Vienna he passed the Hessian armies marching to France. In 1796 and 1797 he set the war poems of Friedberg to music : a Song of Farewell, and a patriotic chorus; *Ein grosses deutches Volk sind wir* (A great German people are we). But it was in vain that he sang of the enemies of the Revolution ; the Revolution overcame the world—and Beethoven with it. From 1798, in spite of the strained relations between Austria and France, Beethoven became closely connected with the French, with the Embassy and General Bernadotte, who had just arrived in Vienna. In this intercourse strong republican sympathies showed themselves in Beethoven, and these feelings became stronger and stronger with time.

A sketch which Steinhauser made of him at this time gives a good idea of his general appearance at this period. This portrait of Beethoven is to later ones what Guérin's portrait of Napoleon is to the other effigies. Guérin's face is rugged, almost savage, and wasted with ambition. Beethoven looks very young for his age, thin and straight, very stiff in his high cravat, a defiant, strained look in his eyes; he knows his own worth and is confident of his power. In 1796 he wrote in his notebook, "Courage! in spite of all my bodily weakness my genius shall yet triumph. . . . Twenty-five years ! that is my age now. . . . This very year the man I am, must reveal himself entirely."[1] Both Madame von Bernhard and Gelinck say that he was extremely proud with rough and clumsy ways and spoke with a strong provincial accent. Only his intimate friends knew what exquisite talent lay hidden under this rough exterior. Writing to Wegeler about his successes, the first thought that springs to his mind is the following : " for example, I meet a friend in need; if my purse does not allow me to help him at once, I have only to go to my work table, and in a short time I have removed his trouble. . . See how charming it is to do this."[2] And a little further on, he says : " My art shall be devoted to no other object than the relief of the poor " (*Dann soll meine Kunst sich nur zum Besten der Armen zeigen*).

Trouble was already knocking at the door; it entered—never more to leave him. Between 1796 and 1800, deafness began its sad work. He suffered from continual singing and humming in his ears.[3] His hearing became gradually weaker.

1 It can hardly be called his début, for his first Concert in Vienna had taken place on 30th March, 1795.

2 To Wegeler, 29th June, 1801 (Nohl 14). " None of my friends shall want whilst I have anything," he wrote to Ries about 1801.

3 In his Will and Testament of 1802, Beethoven says that his deafness first appeared six years before—very likely in 1796. Le. us notice in passing that in the catalogue of his works, Opus one alone (Three Trios) was written before 1796. Opus 2, the first three Piano Sonatas appeared in March, 1796. It may, therefore, be said that the whole of Beethoven's work is that of a deaf man.

See the article on Beethoven's deafness by Dr. Klotz Forest

For several years he kept the secret to himself,
even from his dearest friends. He avoided com-
pany, so that his infliction should not be noticed.
But in 1801 he can no longer remain silent; and
in his despair he confides in two of his friends,
Dr. Wegeler and Pastor Amenda. "My dear,
good, loving Amenda, how often have I longed to
have you near me! Your Beethoven is very unhappy. You must know that the best part of
me, my hearing, has become very weak. Even at
the time when we were together I was aware of
distressing symptoms which I kept to myself; but
my condition is now much worse. . . . . Can I ever
be cured? Naturally I hope so; but my hopes
are very faint, for such maladies are the least
hopeful of all. How sad my life is! For I am
obliged to avoid all those I love and all that are
dear to me; and all this in a world so miserable
and so selfish! . . . . How sad is this resignation
in which I take refuge! Of course I have steeled

in the "Medical Chronicle" of 15th May, 1905. The writer of
the article believes that the complaint had its origin in a general
hereditary affliction (perhaps in the phthisis of his mother). The
deafness increased without ever becoming total. Beethoven
heard low sounds better than high ones. In his last years it is
said that he used a wooden rod, one end of which was placed in
the piano sound-box, the other between his teeth. He used this
means of hearing when he composed.

(On the same question see C. G. Cunn: *Wiener medizinische
Wochenschrift*, February-March, 1892; Nagel: *Die Musik* (15th
March, 1902); Theodor von Frimmel: *Der Merker*, July, 1912).

There are preserved in the Beethoven museum at Bonn the
acoustical instruments made for Beethoven, about 1814, by the
mechanician Maelzel.

myself to rise above all these misfortunes. But how is this going to be possible ?[1] . . . ." And to Wegeler : " . . . . I lead a miserable life indeed. For the last two years I have completely avoided all society, for I cannot talk with my fellow-men. I am deaf. Had my profession been any other, things might still be bearable; but as it is, my situation is terrible. What will my enemies say ? And they are not few ! . . . . At the theatre I always have to be quite near the orchestra in order to understand the actor. I cannot hear the high notes of the instruments or the voices, if I am but a little distance off. . . . . When anyone speaks quietly I only hear with difficulty, ... On the other hand, I find it unbearable when people shout to me. . . . . Often I have cursed my very existence. Plutarch has guided me to a spirit of resignation. If it be possible at all, I will courageously bear with my fate ; but there are moments in my life when I feel the most miserable of all God's creatures. . . . Resignation ! What a sorry refuge ! And yet it is the only one left to me !"

This tragic sadness is expressed in some of the works of this period, in the *Sonate pathétique* Op. 13 (1799), and especially in the *Largo* of the Piano Sonata in D, Opus 10, No. 3 (1798). It is a

1 I have translated these extracts from M. Rolland's text. Mr. Shedlock's translation from the original German may be seen on pages 65 *et seq.*—B.C.H.

marvel that we do not find it in all the works;
the radiant Septet (1800), the limpid First Symphony (C Major, 1800), both breathe a spirit of
youthful gaiety.   There is no doubt that he is
determined to accustom his soul to grief.   The
spirit of man has such a strong desire for happiness that when it has it not, it is forced to create
it. When the present has become too painful, the
soul lives on the past. Happy days are not ef-
faced at one stroke. Their radiance persists long
after they have gone.   Alone and unhappy in
Vienna, Beethoven took refuge in the remembrances of his native land; his thoughts were
always of Bonn. The theme of the *Andante* for
the Variation in the *Septet* is a Rhenish Song.
The Symphony in C Major is also inspired by
the Rhine. It is a poem of youth smiling over its
own dreams. It is gay and languorous; one feels
there the hope and the desire of pleasing. But in
certain passages in the Introduction, in the shad-
ing of the sombre bass passages of the *Allegro,* in
this young composer, in the fantastic *Scherzo,* one
feels with emotion the promise of the great genius
to come. The expression calls to mind the
eyes of Botticelli's *Bambino* in his *Holy Families*
—those eyes of a little child in which one already
divines the approaching tragedy.

Troubles of another kind were soon to be added
to his physical sufferings. Wegeler says that he
never knew Beethoven to be free of a love passion
carried to extremes. These love affairs seemed

to have always been of the purest kind. With
him there was no connection between passion and
pleasure. The confusion established between the
two things nowadays only shows how little most
men know of passion and its extreme rarity.
Beethoven had something of the Puritan in his
nature; licentious conversation and thoughts were
abhorrent to him; he had always unchangeable
ideas on the sanctity of love. . . . . It is said that
he could not forgive Mozart for having prostituted
his genius by writing *Don Giovanni*. Schindler,
who was his intimate friend, assures us that " he
spent his life in virginal modesty without ever
having to reproach himself for any weakness."
Such a man was destined to be the dupe and
victim of love; and so indeed it came about. He
was always falling violently in love and ceaselessly dreaming of its happiness, only however to be
deceived and to be plunged in the deepest suffering. In these alternating states of love and
passionate grief, of youthful confidence and out-
raged pride, we find the most fruitful source of
Beethoven's inspiration, until at length his fiery,
passionate nature gradually calms down into
melancholy resignation.

In 1801 the object of his passion appears to have
been Giulietta Guicciardi, whom he immortalised
in the dedication of the famous (so-called) " Moonlight " Sonata, Opus 27 (1802). " I now see
things in a better light," he writes to Wegeler,
" and associate more with my kind. . . . . This

change has been brought about by the charm of a
dear girl; she loves me and I love her. These
are the first happy moments I have had for two
years."[1] He paid dearly for them. From the
first, this love made him feel more keenly the
misery of the infirmity which had overtaken him
and the precarious conditions of his life which
made it impossible for him to marry the one he
loved. Moreover, Giulietta was a flirt, childish
and selfish by nature; she made Beethoven suffer
most cruelly, and in November 1803, she married
Count Gallenberg.[2] Such passions devastate the
soul; indeed, when the spirit is already enfeebled
by illness, as was Beethoven's, complete disaster
is risked. This was the only time in Beethoven's
life when he seems to have been on the point of
succumbing. He passed the terrible crisis, however, and the details are given in a letter known
as the *Heiligenstadt Testament* to his brothers
Carl and Johann, with the following direction: " To be read and carried out after my
death."[3] It is an outcry of revolt, full of the
most poignant grief. One cannot hear it without

1 To Wegeler, 16 November, 1801.
2 She was not afraid either of boasting of her old love for
Beethoven in preference to that for her husband. Beethoven
helped Gallenberg. " He was my enemy ; that is the very
reason why I should do all possible for him," he told Schindler
on one of his conversation note-books in 1821. But he scorned
to take advantage of the position. " Having arrived in Vienna,"
he wrote in French, " she sought me out and came weeping to
me, but I rejected her."
3 6th October, 1802 (see page 57).

being cut to the heart. In that dark hour he was on the verge of suicide. Only his strong moral force saved him.[1] His final hopes of recovering his health disappeared. " Even the lofty courage which has hitherto sustained me has now disappeared. O Providence, grant that but a single day of real happiness may be mine once again. I have been a stranger to the thrill of joy for so long. When, O God, when shall I feel joy once more ? . . . . Ever again ? No, that would be too cruel ! "

This is indeed a cry of a torn heart, and Beethoven was destined to live yet twenty-five years longer. His powerful nature would not refuse to sink beneath the weight of his woe. " My physical strength improves always with the growth of my intellectual force. . . . . Yes, I really feel that my youth is only just beginning. Each day brings me nearer to my goal, which I can feel without being able to define clearly. . . . . O, if I were only free from my deafness I would embrace the world ! . . . . No rest ! At least, none that I know of except sleep ; and I am so unhappy that I have to give more time to it than formerly. If only I could be free of a part of my

---

1 " Bring up your children to be virtuous. That alone can make them happy ; money will not. I speak from experience. It is that which sustained me in my misery. Virtue and Art alone have saved me from taking my own life." And in another letter, 2nd May, 1810, to Wegeler : " If I had not read somewhere that a man ought not to take his own life so long as he can still do a kind action, I should long ago have ended my existence, and doubtless by my own hand."

infirmity; and then . . . . no, I can bear it no longer. I will wage war against destiny. It shall not overcome me completely. Oh, how fine it would be to live a thousand lives in one!"[1]

This love of his, this suffering, this resignation, these alternations of dejection and pride, these " soul-tragedies " are all reflected in the great compositions written in 1802—the Sonata with the Funeral March, Opus 26; the *Sonata quasi una Fantasia*, Opus 27, No. 1; the Sonata called the " Moonlight," Opus 27; the Sonata in D Minor, Opus 31, No. 2, with its dramatic recitatives which seem like some grand yet heart-broken monologue; the Sonata in C minor for Violin, Opus 30, dedicated to the Emperor Alexander; the Kreutzer Sonata, Opus 47; and the Six Religious Songs, heroic yet grief-laden, to the words of Gellert, Opus 48. The Second Symphony written in 1803 reflects rather his youthful love; and here one feels that his will is decidedly gaining the upper hand An irresistible force sweeps away his sad thoughts, a veritable bubbling over of life shows itself in the finale. Beethoven was determined to be happy. He was not willing to believe his misfortune hopeless, he wanted health, he wanted love, and he threw aside despair.[2]

· · · · · ·

1 To Wegeler.
2 Hornemann's miniature, of 1802, represents Beethoven dressed in the fashion of the day with side whiskers, long hair, the tragic air of one of Byron's heroes, but with the firm Napoleonic look which never gives way.

In many of his works one is struck by the powerful and energetic march rhythms, full of the fighting spirit. This is especially noticeable in the *Allegro* and the *Finale* of Second Symphony, and still more in the first movement, full of superb heroism, of the Violin Sonata dedicated to the Emperor Alexander. The war-like character of this music recalls the period in which it was written. The Revolution had reached Vienna. Beethoven was completely carried away by it. " He spoke freely amongst his intimate friends," said the Chevalier de Seyfried, " on political affairs, which he estimated with unusual intelligence, with a clear and well-balanced out-look. All his sympathies leaned towards revolutionary ideas." He liked the Republican principles. Schindler, the friend who knew him best during the last period of his life, said, " He was an upholder of unlimited liberty and of national independence . . . . . he desired that everyone should take part in the government of the State. . . . . For France he desired universal suffrage and hoped that Bonaparte would establish it, thus laying down the proper basis of human happiness." A Roman of the revolutionary type, brought up on Plutarch, he dreamt of a triumphant Republic, founded by the god of victory, the first Consul. And blow by blow he forged the Eroica Symphony, Bonaparte, 1804,[1] the *Iliad* of Empire, and the Finale

1 It is a fact that the Eroica Symphony was written for and around Bonaparte, and the first MS. still bears the title, " Bonaparte." Afterwards Beethoven learnt of the Coronation of

C

of the Symphony in C minor, 1805 to 1808, the grand epic of glory. This is really the first music breathing the revolutionary feeling. The soul of the times lives again in it with the intensity and purity which great events have for those mighty and solitary souls who live apart and whose impressions are not contaminated by contact with the reality. Beethoven's spirit reveals itself, marked with stirring events, coloured by the reflections of these great wars. Evidences of this, (perhaps unconscious to him) crop up everywhere in the works of this period, in the *Coriolanus* Overture (1807), where tempests roar over the scene; in the Fourth Quartet, Opus 18, the first movement of which shows a close relation to this Overture; in the *Sonata Appassionata*, Op. 57 (1804), of which Bismarck said, "If I heard that

Napoleon. Breaking out into a fury, he cried : " He is only an ordinary man " ; and in his indignation he tore off the dedication and wrote the avenging and touching title : *Sinfonia Eroica composta per festeggiare il souvenire di un grand Uomo.* (Heroic Symphony composed to celebrate the memory of a great man). Schindler relates that later on his scorn for Napoleon became more subdued ; he saw in him rather the unfortunate victim of circumstances worthy of pity, an Icarus flung down from Heaven. When he heard of the St. Helena catastrophe in 1821, he remarked : " I composed the music suitable for this sad event some seventeen years ago." It pleased him to recognise in the Funeral March of his Symphony a presentiment of the conqueror's tragic end. There was then probably in the *Eroica Symphony* and especially in the first movement, a kind of portrait of Bonaparte in Beethoven's mind, doubtless very different from the real man, and rather what he imagined him to be or would have liked him to be—the genius of the Revolution. Beethoven, in the Finale of the Eroica Symphony, used again one of the chief phrases of the work he had already written on the revolutionary hero par excellence, the god of liberty, Prometheus, 1801.

often I should always be very valiant ";[1] in the
score of *Egmont;* and even in his Pianoforte Con-
certos, in the one in E flat, Opus 73 (1809), where
even the virtuosity is heroic: whole armies of
warriors pass by. Nor need we be astonished at
this. Though when writing the Funeral March
on the death of an hero (Sonata, Opus 26), Beethoven was ignorant that the hero most worthy of
his music, namely Hoche, the one who approxi-
mated more closely than Bonaparte to the model
of the *Eroica Symphony,* had just died near the
Rhine, where indeed his tomb stands at the top
of a small hill between Coblentz and Bonn. . . . .
He had twice seen the Revolution victorious in
Vienna itself. French officers were present at the
first production of *Fidelio* in Vienna in November,
1805. It was General Hulin, the conqueror of the
Bastille, who stayed with Lobkovitz, Beethoven's
friend and protector, to whom he dedicated the
Eroica and the C minor Symphony. And on
10 May, 1809, Napoleon slept at Schönbrunn.[2]

. . . . . .

1 Robert de Keudell, German Ambassador in Rome: *Bismarck
and his family,* 1901. Robert de Keudell played this Sonata to
Bismarck on an indifferent piano on 30th October, 1870, at
Versailles. Bismarck remarked regarding the latter part of the
work: " The sighs and struggles of a whole life are in this
music." He preferred Beethoven to all other composers, and
more than once affirmed " Beethoven's music more than any
other soothes my nerves."

2 Beethoven's house was situated near those fortifications of
Vienna which Napoleon had blown up after the taking of the
city. " What an awful life, with ruins all around me," wrote
Beethoven to the publishers, Breitkopf & Härtel, on 26th June,
1809 " nothing but drums, trumpets, and misery of every kind,"

Beethoven suddenly broke off the C minor Symphony to write the Fourth Symphony at a single sitting without his usual sketches. Happiness had come to him. In May 1806, he was betrothed to Theresa von Brunswick.[1] She had loved him for a long time—ever since as a young girl she had taken piano lessons from him during his first stay in Vienna. Beethoven was a friend of her brother Count Franz. In 1806 he stayed with them at Martonvasar in Hungary, and it was there that they fell in love. The remembrance of these happy days is kept fresh by some stories in some of Theresa's writings.[2]   " One Sunday even-

A portrait of Beethoven at this time has been left to us by a Frenchman who saw him in Vienna in 1809, Baron Trémont, of the Council of State. It gives a picturesque description of the disorder in Beethoven's room. They talked together of philosophy, religion, politics, and " especially of Shakespeare." Beethoven was very much inclined to follow Trémont to Paris, where he knew they had already performed his Symphonies at the Conservatoire, and there he had many enthusiastic admirers. (See Mercure Musical, 1 May, 1906, Une visite à Beethoven, by Baron Trémont, published by J. Chantavoine).

1 Or to be more exact, Theresa Brunsvik. Beethoven had met the Brunsviks at Vienna between 1796 and 1799. Giulietta Guicciardi was the cousin of Theresa. Beethoven seems also to have been attracted at one period by one of Theresa's sisters, Josephine, who first married Count Deym, and later on, the Baron Stackelberg. Some very striking details on the Brunsvik family are found in an article by M. André de Hevesy. Beethoven et l'Immortelle Bien-aimée (Revue de Paris, March 1 and 15, 1910). For this study M. de Hevesy has made use of the MS. Memoires and the papers of Theresa, which were preserved at Martonvasar in Hungary. They all show an affectionate intimacy between Beethoven and the Brunsviks, and raise again the question of his love for Theresa. But the arguments are not convincing, and I leave them to be discussed at some future time.

2 Marian Tenger : Beethovens unsterbliche Geliebte (Beethoven's undying Love), Bonn, 1890.

ing " she says, " after dinner, with the moon
shining into the room, Beethoven was seated at the
piano. At first he laid his hands flat on the key-
board. Franz and I always understood this, for it
was his usual preparation. Then he struck some
chords in the bass and slowly with an air of solem-
nity and mystery drifted into a song of John
Sebastian Bach : ' *If thou wilt give me thy heart,
first let it be in secret, that our hearts may com-
mingle and no one divine it.*'[1] My mother and the
priest had fallen asleep and my brother was dream
gazing whilst I who understood his song and his
expression, felt life come to me in all its fullness.
The following morning we met in the park and he
said to me, ' I am now writing an opera ; the principal character is in me and around me wherever I
go. Never before have I reached such heights of
happiness ; I feel light, purity and splendour all
around me and within. Until now I have been
like the child in the fairy story, picking up pebbles
along the road without seeing the beautiful flower
blossoming close by.' . . . . It was in May, 1806,
that I became betrothed to him with the ready
consent of my dear brother Franz.

The *Fourth Symphony* composed in this year
is a pure fragrant flower which treasures up the
perfume of these days, the calmest in all his life.
It has been justly remarked that at this time
" Beethoven's desire was to reconcile his genius as

1 *Wilst du dein Herz mir schenken (Aria di Govannini)*, Edition
Peters, 2071. This beautiful air appears in the album which
Bach wrote for his wife, Anna Magdalena.

far as possible with what was generally known and admired in the forms handed down by his predecessors.[1]"

The same conciliating spirit springing from this love re-acted on his manners and his way of living in general. Ignaz von Seyfried and Grillparzar say that he was full of life, bright, happy and witty, courteous in society, patient with tedious people and careful in his dress. Even his deafness was not noticed, and they say that he was in good health with the exception of his eyesight, which was rather weak.[2] This strikes one in looking at Mahler's portrait of him painted at this time, in which he is represented with an elegance unusual for him and a romantic, even slightly affected look. Beethoven wishes to please, and rather fancies himself in doing so. The lion is in love; he draws in his claws. But one feels deep beneath under all this playfulness, the imagination and tenderness of the Symphony in B flat, the tremendous force, the capricious humour and the passionate temper of his nature.

This profound peace was not destined to last although love exercised its soothing influence until

---

1 Nohl : *Life of Beethoven.*
2 Beethoven was really short-sighted. Ignaz von Seyfried says that this was caused by smallpox, and that he was obliged to wear spectacles when quite young. This short-sightedness would probably exaggerate the wild expression of his eyes. His letters between 1823-4 contain frequent complaints on the subject of his eyes which were often painful. See the articles by Christian Kalischer on this subject, *Beethovens Augens und Augenleiden (Die Musik,* 15th March—1s. April, 1902).

1810. Beethoven doubtless owed to it the self-mastery which at this period enabled him to produce some of the most perfect fruits of his genius; that great classical tragedy, the Symphony in C minor and that delicious idyll of a summer's day : the Pastoral Symphony, 1808.[1] The Sonata Appassionata, inspired by Shakespeare's *Tempest*,[2] the Sonata which he himself regarded as his most powerful one, appeared in 1807 and was dedicated to Theresa's brother. To Theresa herself he dedicated the dreamy and fantastic Sonata in F sharp, Opus 78 (1809). An undated letter[3] addressed to his " Immortal Beloved " expresses the intensity of his love no less strongly than does the *Sonata Appassionata*.

July (1806 ?).

" My Angel, my all, my very self.

Just a few words to-day—and indeed in pencil (with thine). Only till to-morrow is my room definitely engaged. What an unworthy waste of time in such matters! Why this deep sorrow where necessity speaks? Can our love endure otherwise than through sacrifices, through restraint in longing? Canst thou help not being wholly mine? Can I, not being wholly thine? Oh! gaze at nature in all

---

[1] The music for Goethe's play *Egmont* was commenced in 1809. Beethoven had also wished to write the music to William Tell, but Gyrovetz was chosen before him.

[2] Conversation with Schindler.

[3] But written (so it seems) from Korompa at the Brunswick's house.

its beauty, and calmly accept the inevitable—
love demands everything, and rightly so. Thus
is it for me with thee, for thee with me, only
thou so easily forgettest that I must live for myself and for thee. Were we wholly united, thou
wouldst feel this painful fact as little as I should.
My journey was terrible. I arrived here only
yesterday morning at four o'clock, and as they
were short of horses, the mail-coach selected
another route; but what an awful road! At
the last stage but one, I was advised not to
travel by night; they warned me against the
wood, but that only spurred me on, and I was
wrong; the coach must needs break down, the
road being dreadful, a swamp, a mere country
road; without the postillions I had with me I
should have stuck on the way. Esterhazy, by
the ordinary road, met the same fate with eight
horses as I with four—yet it gave me some
pleasure, as successfully overcoming any difficulty always does. Now for a quick change
from without to within; we shall probably soon
see each other; besides, to-day I cannot tell thee
what has been passing through my mind during
the past few days concerning my life. Were
our hearts closely united I should not do things
of this kind. My heart is full of the many
things I have to say to thee. Ah! there are
moments in which I feel that speech is power-
less. Cheer up. Remain my true, my only
treasure, my all! ! ! As I to thee. The gods

must send the rest; what is in store for us must
be and ought to be.

Thy faithful
LUDWIG."

It is difficult to divine what was the barrier
which separated these two from the consummation
of their love. Was it the lack of fortune or the
difference in social position? Perhaps Beethoven
rebelled against the long period of probation
which was imposed on him or resented the humiliation of keeping his love secret for an indefinite
period. Perhaps, impulsive and afflicted as he
was, a misanthrope too, he caused his loved one
to suffer without wishing it and gave himself up
to despair in consequence. The fact remains that
the engagement was broken off, although neither
seems ever to have proved faithless.

Even to her last day (she lived till 1861) Theresa
von Brunswick loved Beethoven, and Beethoven
was no less faithful. In 1816 he remarked,
" When I think of her my heart beats as violently
as on the day when I first saw her." To this year
belong the six songs, Opus 98, which have so
touching and profound a feeling. They are dedicated " To the loved one far away " (An die ferne
Geliebte). He wrote in his notes, " My heart
overflows at the thought of her beautiful nature;
and yet she is not here, not near me!" Theresa
had given her portrait to Beethoven, inscribed,
" To the rare genius, the great artist, the generous

man. T.B."[1] Once during the last year of his life a friend surprised Beethoven alone, and found him holding this portrait and speaking to himself through his tears : " Thou wert so lovely and great, so like to an angel !" The friend withdrew, and returning a little later found him at the piano, and said " To-day, my old friend, there are no black looks on your face." Beethoven replied " It is because my good angel has visited me." The wound was deep. " Poor Beethoven " he said to himself, " there is no happiness for you in this world; only in the realms of the ideal will you find strength to conquer yourself."[2]

In his notebook he wrote, " submission, complete submission to your destiny. You can no longer live for yourself, only for others. For you there is happiness only in your art. O God, give me strength to conquer " myself." ' " . . .

. . . . . .

Love then abandoned him. In 1810 he was once more alone; but joy had come to him and the consciousness of his power. He was in the prime of life. He gave himself up to his violent and wild moods regardless of results, and certainly without care for the opinions of the world and the

---

1 This portrait can still be seen in Beethoven's house at Bonn. It is reproduced in Frimmel's *Life of Beethoven*, page 29, and in the " Musical Times," 15th December, 1892.
2 To Gleichenstein.

usual conventions of life. What, indeed, had he
to fear or to be careful of? Gone are love and
ambition. Strength and the joy of it, the necessity for using it, almost abusing it, were left to him.
" Power constitutes the morality of men who dis-
tinguish themselves above the ordinary." He
returned to his neglect in matters of dress, and his
manners now became even freer than before. He
knew that he had the right to speak freely even to
the greatest. " I recognise no sign of superiority
in mankind other than goodness," he writes on 17
July, 1812.[1] Bettina Brentano, who saw him at that
time, says that " no king or emperor was ever so
conscious of his power." She was fascinated by
his very strength. " When I saw him for the
first time," she wrote to Goethe, " the whole exterior world vanished from me. Beethoven made
me forget the world, and even you, O Goethe. . . .
I do not think I am wrong in saying this man is
very far ahead of modern civilisation." Goethe
attempted to make Beethoven's acquaintance.[2]

1 " The heart is the mainspring of all that is great " (to
Giannatasio del Rio).

2 " Goethe's poems give me great happiness," he wrote to
Bettina Brentano on 19th February, 1811. And also " Goethe
and Schiller are my favourite poets, together with Ossian and
Homer, whom, unfortunately, I can only read in translations."
To Breitkopf & Härtel, 8th August, 1809, Nohl, New Letters,
LIII.

It is remarkable that Beethoven's taste in literature was so
sound in view of his neglected education. In addition to Goethe,
who he said was " grand, majestic, always in D major " (and
more than Goethe) he loved three men, Homer, Plutarch and
Shakespeare. Of Homer's works he preferred the Odyssey to
the Iliad; he was continually reading Shakespeare (from a

They met at a Bohemian spa, Töplitz, in 1812, but did not agree well. Beethoven passionately admired Goethe's genius; but his own character was too free and too wild not to wound the susceptibilities of Goethe. Beethoven himself has told us of this walk which they took together, in the course of which the haughty republican gave the courtly councillor of the Grand-duke of Weimar a lesson in dignity which he never forgot.

" Kings and princes can easily make professors and privy councillors; they can bestow titles and decorations, but they cannot make great men, or minds which rise above the base turmoil of this world . . . . and when two men are together such as Goethe and myself these fine gentlemen must be made conscious of the difference between ourselves and them. Yesterday, as we were returning home on foot, we met the whole of the Imperial family. We saw them approaching from a distance. Goethe let go my arm to take his stand by the road side with the crowd. It was in vain that I talked to him. Say what I would I could not get him to move a single step. I drew my hat down upon my

German translation) and we know with what tragic grandeur he has set *Coriolanus* and the *Tempest* in music. He read Plutarch continually, as did all who were in favour of the revolution. Brutus was his hero, as was also the case with Michael Angelo; he had a small statue of him in his bedroom. He loved Plato, and dreamed of establishing his republic in the whole world. " Socrates and Jesus have been my models," he wrote once on his notebooks (*Conversations during 1819 and*

head, buttoned up my overcoat, and forced my
way through the throng. Princes and courtiers
stood aside. Duke Rudolph raised his hat to
me, the Empress bowing to me first. The great
of the earth know me and recognise me. I
amused myself in watching the procession pass
by Goethe. He remained on the road side bowing low, hat in hand. I took him to task for it
pretty severely and did not spare him at all."[1]
Nor did Goethe forget the scene.[2]

In 1812 the Seventh and Eighth Symphonies

[1] To Bettina von Arnim. The authenticity of Beethoven's
letters to Bettina, doubted by Schindler, Marx and Deiters, has
been supported by Moritz Carriere, Nohl and Kalischer. Bettina
has perhaps embellished them a little, but the foundation remains
reliable.

[2] " Beethoven," said Goethe to Zelter, " is, unfortunately,
possessed of a wild and uncouth disposition ; doubtless, he is
not wrong in finding the world detestable, but that is not the
way to make it pleasant for himself or for others. We must
excuse and pity him for he is deaf." After that he did nothing
against Beethoven nor did he do anything for him, but he
ignored him completely. At the bottom, however, he admired
Beethoven's music and feared it also. He was afraid it would
cause him to lose that mental calm which he had gained through
so much trouble. A letter of young Felix Mendelssohn, who
passed through Weimar in 1830, gives us a very interesting
glimpse into the depths of that storm-tossed passionate soul
controlled as it was by a masterly and powerful intellect. . . .
" At first," writes Mendelssohn, " he did not want to hear
Beethoven's name mentioned, but after a time he was persuaded
to listen to the First Movement of the Symphony in C minor,
which moved him deeply. He would not show anything out-
wardly, but merely remarked to me, ' that does not touch me, it
only surprises me.' After a time he said ' It is really grand,
it is maddening, you would think the house was crumbling to
pieces.' Afterwards, at dinner, he sat pensive and absorbed until
he began to question me about Beethoven's music. I saw quite
clearly that a deep impression had been made on him. . . ."
(For information on the relations between Goethe and Beethoven, see various articles by Frimmel).

were written during a stay of several months at
Töplitz.   These works are veritable orgies of
rhythm and humour; in them he is perhaps re-
vealing himself in his most natural and as he
styled it himself, most " unbuttoned " (aufge-
knopft) moods, transports of gaiety contrasting
unexpectedly with storms of fury and disconcert-
ing flashes of wit followed by those Titanic
explosions which terrified both Goethe and Zelter[1]
and caused the remark in North Germany that the
Symphony in A was the work of a drunkard. The
work of an inebriated man indeed it was, but one
intoxicated with power and genius; one who said
of himself, " I am the Bacchus who crushes delicious nectar for mankind. It is I who give the
divine frenzy to men." Wagner wrote, " I do
not know whether Beethoven wished to depict a
Dionysian orgy[2] in the Finale of his Symphony,
though I recognise in this passionate kermesse a
sign of his Flemish origin, just as we see it likewise in his bold manner of speech and in his
bearing so free and so utterly out of harmony with
a country ruled by an iron discipline and rigid
etiquette. Nowhere is there greater frankness or
freer power than in the Symphony in A. It is a

1 Letter from Goethe to Zelter, 2nd September, 1812. . . .
Zelter to Goethe, 14th September, 1812 : " Auch ich bewundere
ihn mit Schrecken " (" I, too, regard him with mingled admiration and dread "). Zelter writes to Goethe in 1819, " They
say he is mad."
2 At any rate, this was a subject which Beethoven had in
his mind; for we find it in his notes, especially those for the
proposed Tenth Symphony,

mad outburst of superhuman energy, with no other object than for the pleasure of unloosing it like a river overflowing its banks and flooding the surrounding country. In the Eighth Symphony the power is not so sublime, though it is still more strange and characteristic of the man, mingling tragedy with farce and a Herculean vigour with the games and caprices of a child."[1]

The year 1814 marks the summit of Beethoven's fortunes. At the Vienna Congress he enjoyed European fame. He took an active part in the fêtes, princes rendered him homage, and (as he afterwards boasted to Schindler) he allowed himself to be courted by them. He was carried away by his sympathy with the War of Independence.[2] In 1813 he wrote a Symphony on *Wellington's Victory* and in the beginning of 1814 a martial chorus, *Germany's Rebirth (Germanias Wiedergeburt)*. On November 29th, 1814, he conducted before an audience of kings a patriotic Cantata, *The Glorious Moment (Der glorreiche Augenblick)*, and on the occasion of the capture of Paris in 1815 he composed a Chorus, *It is accomplished (Es ist vollbracht)*. These occasional pieces did more to spread his fame than all the rest of his music together. The engraving by Blasius Hoefel

[1] There was a very tender intimacy between Amalie Sebald and him about this time, and it is possible that this may have supplied the inspiration.

[2] Differing from him in this, Schubert had written in 1807 a *pièce d'occasion*, in honour of Napoleon the Great, and conducted the performance himself before the Emperor.

from a sketch by the Frenchman Latronne and the savage-looking cast by Franz Klein in 1812 present a lifelike image of Beethoven at the time of the Congress of Vienna. The dominating characteristic of this leonine face with its firm set jaws scored with the furrows of anger and trouble, is determination—a Napoleonic will. One recognises the man who said of Napoleon after Jena, " How unfortunate that I do not know as much about warfare as music! I would show myself his master." But his kingdom was not of this world. " My empire is in the air," he wrote to Franz von Brunswick.[1]

.   .   .   .   .   .

After this hour of glory comes the saddest and most miserable period. Vienna had never been sympathetic to Beethoven. Haughty and bold genius as he was, he could not be at ease in this frivolous city with its mundane and its mediocre spirit, which Wagner laughed to scorn later on.[2] He lost no opportunities of going away; and

[1] " I say nothing of our monarchs and their kingdoms,'' he wrote to Kauka during the Congress. " To my mind, the empire of the spirit is the dearest of all. It is the first of all kingdoms, temporal and spiritual."

[2] Vienna, is that not to say everything? All trace of German Protestantism eradicated, even the national accent lost, Italianised. . . . . German spirit, German habits and ways explained from textbooks of Italian and Spanish origin. . . . . The country of debased history, falsified science, falsified religion. . . . A frivolous scepticism calculated to undermine all love of truth, honour, and independence! (Wagner, *Beethoven*, 1870).

Grillparzer has written that it was a misfortune to be born an Austrian. The great German composers of the end of the 19th Century who have lived in Vienna, have suffered cruelly

towards 1808 he thought seriously of leaving
Austria to go to the court of Jerome Bonaparte,
King of Westphalia.[1] But Vienna had abundant
musical resources; and one must do it justice by
saying that there were always noble *dilettanti* who
felt the grandeur of Beethoven, and who spared
their country the shame of losing him. In 1809,
three of the richest noblemen of Vienna, the Archduke Rudolph, a pupil of Beethoven, Prince
Lobkovitz and Prince Kinsky undertook to pay
him annually a pension of 4,000 florins on the sole
condition that he remained in Austria. " As it is
evident," they said, " that a man can only devote
himself entirely to art when he is free from all
material care, and that it is only then that he can
produce such sublime works which are the glory of
art, the undersigned have formed a resolution to
release Ludwig van Beethoven from the shadow of
need, and thus disperse the miserable obstacles
which are so detrimental to his flights of genius."
Unhappily the results did not come up to the
promises. The pension was always very irregularly paid; soon it ceased altogether. Also Vienna
had very much changed in character after the

from the spirit of this town, delivered up to the Pharisaical cult
of Brahms. The life of Bruckner was one long martyrdom.
Hugo Wolf, who battled furiously before giving in, has uttered
implacable judgments on Vienna.

1 King Jerome had offered Beethoven an annuity of six hundred
ducats of gold and 150 silver ducats for travelling expenses, for
playing to him occasionally and for managing his chamber-music
concerts, which were not long or very frequent. Beethoven was
eager to go.

D

Congress of 1814. Society was distracted from art by politics. Musical taste was spoilt by Italianism, and the fashionable people favoured Rossini, treating Beethoven as pedantic.[1] Beethoven's friends and protectors went away or died : Prince Kinsky in 1812, Lichnovsky in 1814, Lobkovitz in 1816. Rasumowsky, for whom he had written the three admirable Quartets, Opus 59, gave his last concert in February, 1815. In 1815 Beethoven quarrelled with Stephen von Breuning, the friend of his childhood, the brother of Eleonore.[2] From this time he was alone.[3] " I have no friends. I am alone in the world " he wrote in his notebook of 1816.

His deafness became complete.[4] After the

---

1 Rossini's *Tancredi* sufficed to shake the whole German musical edifice. Bauernfold (quoted by Ehrhard) notes in his *Journal* this criticism which circulated in the Viennese salons in 1816: " Mozart and Beethoven are old pedants; the stupidity of the preceding period amused them : it is only since Rossini that one has really known melody. *Fidelio* is quite devoid of music; one cannot understand why people take the trouble to weary themselves with it." Beethoven gave his last concert as pianist in 1814.

2 The same year Beethoven lost his brother Karl. " He clung to life so, that I would willingly have given mine," he wrote to Antonia Brentano.

3 Except for his intimate friendship with Countess Maria von Erdödy, a constant sufferer like himself, afflicted with an incurable malady. She lost her only son suddenly in 1816. Beethoven dedicated to her in 1809 his two Trios Op. 70 ; and in 1815-17, his two great Sonatas for Violoncello Op. 102.

4 Besides his deafness, his health grew worse from day to day. During October, 1816, he was very ill. In the summer of 1817 his doctor said he had a chest complaint. During the winter, 1817-18, he was tormented with his so-called phthisis. Then he had acute rheumatism in 1820-21, jaundice in 1821, and several maladies in 1823.

autumn of 1815 he could only communicate with
his friends by writing.[1] The oldest conversation-
book is dated 1816.[2] There is a sad story recorded
by Schindler with regard to the representation of
Fidelio in 1822. " Beethoven wanted to conduct
the general rehearsal. . . . . From the duet of the
First Act, it was evident that he could hear nothing of what was going on. He kept back the
pace considerably; and whilst the orchestra followed his beat, the singer hurried the time. There
followed general confusion. The usual leader of
the orchestra, Umlauf, suggested a short rest,
without giving any reason; and after exchanging
a few words with the singers, they began again.
The same disorder broke out afresh. Another
interval was necessary. The impossibility of con-
tinuing under Beethoven's direction was evident;
but how could they make him understand? No
one had the heart to say to him, ' Go away, poor
unfortunate one, you cannot conduct.' Beethoven,
uneasy and agitated, turned from side to side,
trying to read the expression of the different faces,
and to understand what the difficulty was : a
silence came over all. Suddenly he called me in
his imperious manner. When I was quite near to
him, he handed me his pocket-book, and made
signs to me to write. I put down these words :

1 A change of style in his music, beginning with the Sonata
Op : 101, dates from this time.
2 Beethoven's conversation-books form more than 11,000 manuscript pages, and can be found bound to-day in the Imperial
Library at Berlin.

' I beg you not to continue; I will explain why at your house.' With one leap he jumped from the platform, saying to me, ' Let us go quickly.' He ran straight to his house, went in and threw himself down on a sofa, covering his face with his hands; he remained like that until dinner-time. At the table it was impossible to draw a word from him; he wore an expression of complete despondency and profound grief. After dinner when I wanted to leave him, he kept me, expressing a desire not to be left alone. When we separated he asked me to go with him to his doctor, who had a great reputation for complaints of the ear. During the whole of my connection with Beethoven I do not know of any day which can compare with this awful day of November. He had been smitten to the heart, and until the day of his death, he retained the impression of this terrible scene.''[1]

Two years later, on 7 May, 1824, when conducting the *Choral Symphony* (or rather, as the programme said, " taking part in the direction of the concert ") he heard nothing at all of the clamour of the audience applauding him. He did not even suspect it, until one of the singers, taking him by the hand turned him round; and he suddenly saw the audience waving their hats and clapping their hands. An English traveller,

1 Schindler, who had been intimate with Beethoven since 1819, had known him slightly since 1814; but Beethoven had found it very difficult to be friendly; he treated him at first with disdainful haughtiness.

Russell, who saw him at the piano about the year
1825, says that when he wanted to play quietly the
notes did not sound and that it was very moving
to follow in silence the emotion animating him
expressed in his face, and in the movements of his
fingers. Buried in himself,[1] and separated from
all mankind, his only consolation was in Nature.
" She was his sole confident," says Theresa of
Brunswick, " she was his refuge." Charles Neate,
who knew him in 1815, says that he never saw
anyone who loved flowers, clouds and nature so
devotedly[2]; he seemed to live in them. " No one
on earth can love the country so much as I,"
wrote Beethoven. " I love a tree more than a
man." When in Vienna he walked round the
ramparts every day. In the country from day-
break till night he walked alone, without hat, in
sunshine or rain. " Almighty God ! In the
woods I am happy, happy in the woods, where
each tree speaks through Thee. O God, what
splendour ! In the forests, on the hills, it is the
calm, the quiet, that helps me."

His unrestfulness of mind found some respite
there.[3] He was harassed by financial cares. He

1 See the admirable notes of Wagner on Beethoven's deafness
(*Beethoven*, 1870).

2 He loved animals and pitied them. The mother of the his-
torian, von Frimmel, says that for a long while she had an
involuntary dislike for Beethoven, because when she was a little
girl he drove away with his handkerchief all the butterflies that
she wanted to catch.

3 He was always uncomfortable in his lodgings. In thirty-five
years in Vienna, he changed his rooms thirty times.

wrote in 1818, " I am almost reduced to beggary, and I am obliged to pretend that I do not lack necessities"; and at another time, " The *Sonata Op. 106* has been written under pressing circumstances. It is a hard thing to have to work for bread." Spohr says that often he could not go out on account of his worn-out shoes. He owed large debts to his publishers and his compositions did not bring him in anything. The *Mass in D,* published by subscription, obtained only seven subscribers (of whom not one was a musician).[1] He received barely thirty or forty ducats for his fine Sonatas, each one of which cost him three months' work. The Quartets, *Opp.* 127, 130, and 132, amongst his profoundest works, which seem to be written with his very heart-blood, were written for Prince Galitzin, who neglected to pay for them. Beethoven was worn out with domestic difficulties, and with endless law suits to obtain the pensions owing to him or to retain the guardianship of a nephew, the son of his brother Carl, who died of consumption in 1815.

He had bestowed on this child all the care and devotion with which his heart overflowed. But he was repaid with cruel suffering. It seemed that a kind of special fate had taken care to renew ceaselessly and to accumulate his miseries in order that his genius should not lack for food. At first he

---

1 Beethoven had written personally to Cherubini, who was " of all his contemporaries the one whom he most esteemed." Cherubini did not reply.

had a dispute over Carl with his mother, who
wanted to take him away. " O, my God," he
cried, " my shield and my defence, my only refuge ! Thou readest the depths of my soul and
Thou knowest the griefs that I experience when
I have to cause suffering to those who want to
dispute my Carl, my treasure.[1] Hearken unto
me, Great Being, that I know not how to name.
Grant the fervent prayer of the most unhappy of
Thy creatures ! "

" O God, aid me ! Thou wilt not leave me entirely in the hands of men ; because I do not wish
to make a covenant with injustice ! Hear the
prayer which I make to Thee, that at least for
the future I may live with my Carl ! . . . . O
cruel fate, implacable destiny ! No, no, my unhappiness will never end ! "

Then this nephew, so passionately loved, proved
unworthy of the confidence of his uncle. The
correspondence between Beethoven and him is sad
and revolting, like that of Michael Angelo with
his brothers, but more simple and touching.

" Am I to be repaid once again with the most
abominable ingratitude ? Ah, well, if the bond
must be broken, so be it ! All impartial people
who hear of it will hate you. If the compact between us weighs too heavily, in the name of God,
may it be according to His will ! I abandon

---

1 " I never avenge myself," he wrote besides to Madame
Streicher. " When I am obliged to act against others, I only
do what is necessary to defend myself or to prevent them from
doing one harm."

you to Providence; I have done all that I
could; I am ready to appear before the Su-
preme Judge!

"Spoilt as you are, that should not make it
difficult to teach you to be simple and true; my
heart has suffered so much by your hypocritical
conduct, and it is difficult for me to forget. . . . .
God is my witness, I only long to be a thousand
miles from you and from that sorry brother and
from this abominable family. . . . . I shall never
more have confidence in you." And he signed
"Unhappily your father—or rather, not your
father." But pardon came almost immediately.

"My dear son! No more of this! Come to
my arms. You shall not hear one harsh word.
I will receive you with the same love. We will
talk over what is to be done for your future in
a friendly manner. On my word of honour there
will be no reproach. That would do no good.
You have nothing to expect from me but sympathy and the most loving care. Come, come to
the faithful heart of your father. Come immediately you receive this letter, come to the house."
(And on the envelope in French, "If you do not
come, you will surely kill me.")

"Do not deceive me," he begged, "be always
my beloved son. What a horrible discord it would
be if you were to be false to me, as many persons
maintain that you already are. . . . Good-bye, he
who has not given you life but who has certainly
preserved it, and who has taken all possible care

BEETHOVEN
AT THE AGE OF 48.

(From a Painting by Kloeber.)

[*To face page* 40.

with your moral development, with an affection
more than paternal, begs you from the bottom of
his heart to follow the only true path of the good
and the just.

Your faithful foster-father.[1]

After having cherished all kinds of dreams for
the future of this nephew, who was not lacking
in intelligence and whom he wished to take up
a University career, Beethoven had to consent to
make a merchant of him. But Carl frequented
gambling dens and contracted debts. By a sad
phenomenon, more frequent than one believes, the
moral grandeur of his uncle, instead of doing him
good, made him worse. It exasperated him, im-
pelling him to revolt, as he said in those terrible
words where his miserable soul appears so plainly,
" I have become worse because my uncle wished
me to do better." He reached such a state that
in the summer of 1826 he shot himself in the head
with a pistol. He did not die from it, but it was
Beethoven who just missed dying. He never recovered from this terrible fright.[2] Carl recovered;
he lived to the end to cause suffering to his uncle,

1 A letter which has been found in Berlin to M. Kalischer,
shews with what deep feeling Beethoven wished to make his
nephew " a citizen useful to the state " (February 1st, 1819).

2 Schindler, who saw him then, says that he suddenly became
an old man of seventy, utterly crushed and broken of will. He
would have died had Carl died. He died soon afterwards.

whose death he hastened in no slight measure.
Nor was he with him at the hour of his death.
"God has never abandoned me," wrote Beethoven
to his nephew, some years before. " He will find
someone to close my eyes." This was not to be
the one whom he called " his son."[1]

.   .   .   .   .   .

It was from the depth of this abyss that Beethoven undertook to chant his immortal *Ode to
Joy* It was the plan of his whole life. As early as
1793, he had thought of it at Bonn.[2] All his life
he wished to celebrate Joy ; and to make it the
climax of one of his great works. He was always
striving to find the exact form of the Hymn, and
the work where he could place it. He was far
from being decided, even in his *Ninth Symphony.*

1 The dilettantism of our time has not failed to seek to re-
instate this scoundrel. This is not surprising.

2 Letter from Fischenich to Charlotte Schiller (January, 1793).
Schiller's Ode was written in 1785. The actual theme appeared
in 1808 in the *Fantasy for piano, orchestra and Choir, Op.* 80,
and in 1810 in the Song on Goethe's words : *Kleine Blumen,
Kleine Blaetter.* I have seen in a note book of 1812 belonging
to Dr Erich Prieger at Bonn, between the sketches of the
Seventh Symphony and a plan for an *Overture to Macbeth,* an
attempt to adopt some words of Schiller to the theme which
he used later on in the *Overture Op.* 115 (*Namensfeier*).
Several instrumental motives of the *Ninth Symphony* appeared
before 1815. Thus the definite theme of Joy was put down in
notes in 1822 ; also all the other airs of the *Symphony,* except
the Trio, which came a little after, then the *andante moderato,*
and later the *adagio,* which appeared last of all. For references
to Schiller's poem and the false interpretation which is given
nowadays by substituting for the word *Joy* the word
Liberty, see an article by Charles Andler in *Pages Libres* (July
8, 1905).

Until the very last moment, he was on the point of putting off the *Ode to Joy* to a *Tenth* or *Eleventh Symphony*. One ought to notice that the *Ninth Symphony* is not entitled *Choral Symphony*, as it is now invariably called, but *Symphony with a Final Chorus on the Ode to Joy*. It narrowly missed having another conclusion. In July, 1823, Beethoven still thought of giving it an instrumental *finale*, which he used later on for the quartet Op : 132. Both Czerny and Sonnleithner say that even after the performance in May, 1824, Beethoven had not abandoned this idea.

He found great technical difficulties in introducing the Chorus into the Symphony, as is shown by Beethoven's note-books and his numerous attempts to make the voices enter at another part of the work and in a different manner. In the sketches for the second subject of the *Adagio*[1] he wrote " Perhaps the Chorus could enter conveniently here." But he could not decide to part from his faithful orchestra. "When an idea comes to me," he said, "I hear it on an instrument, never on a voice." So he put back the place for employing voices as late as possible. At first he wanted to give the instruments not only the *recitatives* of the *Finale*[2] but even the Theme of Joy itself.

But we must go still further into the reason of these hesitations and delays. The explanation is

1 Berlin Library.
2 Exactly as if it had words beneath.

very deep. Continually tormented by grief, this
unfortunate man had always aspired to sing the
excellence of Joy; and from year to year he put
off his task, held back ceaselessly by the whirlwind of his passion and grief. It was only at
the very last that he succeeded. But with what
a success!

At the moment when the Theme of Joy appears
for the first time, the orchestra stops abruptly,
thus giving a sudden unexpected character to the
entrance of the Song. And this is a true touch;
this theme is rightly divine. Joy descends from
heaven enveloped in a supernatural calm; it
soothes the suffering with its cool breath; and
the first impression that it makes, is so tender
as it steals into the sorrowing heart, that a friend
of Beethoven has said "One feels inclined to
weep, as one looks into those soft, calm eyes of
his." When the Theme passes first to the voices,
it is the Basses who present it first with a solemn
and rather weighty character. But, little by
little, Joy takes possession of us. It is a real
battle, a fight with sorrow. We can hear the
rhythms of the marching armies. In the ardent
panting song of the tenor, in all these quivering
pages we can almost feel the breath of Beethoven
himself, the rhythm of his breathing and his inspired cries as he wandered across the fields, composing the work, transported by a demoniacal
fury, like King Lear in the middle of a storm.
After the warlike joy comes religious ecstacy.

Then follows a sacred orgy, a very delirium of love. A whole trembling humanity lifts its arms to the sky, utters powerful outcries, rushes forth towards this Joy and clasps it to the heart.

This Titanic work overcame the indifference of the public. The frivolous crowds of Vienna were moved for an instant, but they still favoured Rossini and his Italian operas. Humiliated and saddened, Beethoven was on the point of going to live in London and thought of giving his *Ninth Symphony* there. A second time, as in 1809, some noble friends sent him a petition asking that he would not leave the country. They said " We know that you have written a new composition of sacred music[1] in which you have expressed senti- ments inspired by your profound faith. The supernatural light which penetrates your great soul illumines the work. We know besides that the garland of your inspired symphonies has been increased by an immortal flower. . . . Your absence during these last years has troubled all those whose eyes are turned to you.[2] Everyone sadly thought that the man of genius placed so high amongst living beings remained silent whilst another kind of foreign art sought to plant itself in our country, causing the productions of German art to be forgotten. . . . From you only, the

1 The *Mass in D*, Op : 123.
2 Harassed by domestic quarrels, misery, cares of all kinds, Beethoven only wrote during the five years from 1816 to 1821, three pieces for the piano (Op., 101, 102, and 106). His enemies said he was exhausted. He began to work again in 1821.

nation awaits new life, new laurels, and a new
reign of truth and beauty, despite the fashion of
the day. . . . . Give us the hope of soon seeing
our desires satisfied. And then the springtime
which is coming will blossom again doubly, thanks
to your gifts t us and to the world! "[1] This
noble address shews what power, not only artistic
but also moral, Beethoven exercised over the
élite of Germany. The first word which occurs
to his followers who wish to praise his genius is
neither science, nor art; it is *faith*.[2]

Beethoven was deeply moved by these words.
He stayed. On May 7th, 1824, the first performance in Vienna of the *Mass in D* and the *Ninth
Symphony* took place. The success was amazing;
and his greeting almost of a seditious character
for when Beethoven appeared he was accorded
five rounds of applause; whereas according to the
strict etiquette of the city, it was the custom to
give three only for the entrance of the Royal
Family. The police had to put an end to the
manifestations. The Symphony raised frantic
enthusiasm. Many wept. Beethoven fainted with
emotion after the concert; 'he was taken to

[1] February, 1824. Signed Prince C. Lichnovsky, Count
Maurice Lichnovsky, Count Maurice de Fries, Count M. de
Dietrichstein, Count F. de Palfy, Count Czernin, Ignace Edler
de Mosel, Charles Czerny, Abbé Stadler, A. Diabelli, Artari &
Co., Steiner & Co., A. Streicher, Zmeskall, Kiesewetter, etc.

[2] " My moral character is publicly recognised," Beethoven
proudly said to the Vienna Municipality, on February 1st, 1819,
to vindicate his right to the guardianship of his nephew. Even
distinguished writers like Weisenbach have considered him
worthy of the dedication of their works.

Schindler's house where he remained asleep all the night and the following morning, fully dressed, neither eating nor drinking. The triumph was only fleeting, however, and the concert brought in nothing for Beethoven. His material circumstances of life were not changed by it. He found himself poor, ill,[1] alone but a conqueror[2] : conqueror of the mediocrity of mankind, conqueror of his destiny, conqueror of his suffering. " Sacrifice, always sacrifice the trifles of life to art ! God is over all ! "

.   .   .   .   .   .

He had then completed the object of his whole life. He had tasted perfect Joy. Would he be able to rest on this triumph of the soul which ruled the tempest ? Certainly he ought to feel the relief from the days of his past anguish. Indeed his last quartets are full of strange forebodings. But it seems that the victory of the *Ninth Symphony* had left its glorious traces in its nature. The plans which he had for the future :[3] the *Tenth*

[1] In August, 1824, he was haunted with the fear of sudden death " like my grandfather to whom I bear so much resemblance," he wrote on August 16th, 1824, to Dr. Bach.

[2] The Ninth Symphony was given for the first time in Germany at Frankfurt on April 1st, 1825 ; in London on March 25th, 1825 ; in Paris at the Conservatoire on March 27th, 1831. Mendelssohn, then aged seventeen, gave a performance of it on the piano at the Jaegerhalle in Berlin on November 14th, 1826. Wagner, a student at Leipzig, re-copied it entirely by hand ; and in a letter, dated October 6th, 1830, to the publisher, Schott, offered him a reduction of the Symphony for pianoforte duet. One can say that the Ninth Symphony decided Wagner's career.

[3] " Apollo and his Muses would not wish to deliver me up to death yet, for I still owe them so much. Before I go to the

Symphony,[1] the overture on the name of BACH, the music for Grillparzer's *Melusina,*[2] for Körner's *Odyssey* and Goethe's *Faust,*[3] the Biblical oratorio of *Saul and David,* all shew that he was attracted by the mighty serenity of the old German masters—Bach and Handel—and more still to the light of the South—the South of France or Italy, where he hoped to travel.[4]

Elysian fields I must leave behind me what the spirit inspires and tells me to finish. It seems to me that I have scarcely written anything." (To the brothers Schott, Sept. 17th, 1829.)

1 Beethoven wrote to Moscheles on March 18th, 1827: " The complete sketch of a Symphony is in my desk with a new overture." This sketch has never been found. One only reads in his notes :

" Adagio cantique." Religious song for a symphony in the old modes (*Herr Gott dich loben wir.—Alleluja*), may be in an independent style, may be as introduction to a fugue. This Symphony might be characterised by the entrance of voices, perhaps in the *finale,* perhaps in the *adagio.* The violins in the orchestra, etc., increased ten times for the last movements. The voices to enter one by one ; or to repeat the *adagio* somehow in the last movements. For words for the *adagio,* a Greek myth or an ecclesiastical canticle, in the *allegro,* Bacchus' Feast (1818). As has been seen the choral conclusion was intended to be reserved for a *Tenth Symphony* and not for the *Ninth Symphony.*

Later he said that he wished to accomplish in his *Tenth Symphony* " the reconciliation of the modern world with the ancient, which Goethe had attempted in his *Second Faust.*"

2 The subject is the legend of a horseman who is loved and captured by a fairy, and who suffers from nostalgia and lack of liberty. There are analogies between this poem and that of *Tannhauser.* Beethoven worked at it between 1823 and 1826. (See A. Ehrhard *Franz Grillparzer,* 1900).

3 Since 1808 Beethoven had made plans for writing the music to *Faust.* (The first part of *Faust* appeared under the title of *Tragedy* in the autumn of 1807). It was then his dearest plan.

4 " The South of France ! It is there, there ! " (from a notebook in the Berlin Library). " To go away from here. Only on this sole condition will you be able to rise again to the

Dr. Spiker, who saw him in 1826, said that his face had become smiling and jovial. The same year when Grillparzer spoke to him for the last time, it was Beethoven who had more energy than the worn-out poet : "Ah ! " said the latter, "if I had a thousandth part of your strength and determination." Times were hard; the monarchial reaction oppressed their spirits. "The censors have killed me," groaned Grillparzer. "One must go to North America if one wishes to speak freely." But no power could put a stop to Beethoven's thoughts. "Words are bound in chains, but, happily, sounds are still free," he wrote to the poet Kuffner. Beethoven's is the great voice of freedom, perhaps the only one then of the whole of German thought. He felt it. Often he spoke of the duty which was imposed on him to act by means of his art "for poor humanity, for humanity to come, to restore its courage and to shake off its lassitude and cowardice." "At the present time," he wrote to his nephew, "there is need for mighty spirits to lash into action these wretched rebellious human souls." Dr. Müller said in 1827 that "Beethoven always expressed himself freely on the subjects of government, the police, the aristocracy, even in public. The police knew him but they looked on his criticisms and satires as harmless fancies, and they did not care to interfere with the man whose genius had such

high level of your art. . . A Symphony, then to go away, away, away. The summer to work during a voyage. . . . . Then to travel in Italy and Sicily with some other artist."
E

an extraordinary reputation."[1] Thus nothing was able to break this indomitable will. It seemed now to make sport of grief. The music written in these last years, in spite of the painful circum stances under which it was composed,[2] has often quite a new, ironical character of heroic and joyous disdain. The very last piece that he finished, the new *Finale* to the *Quartet, Op.* 130, is very gay. This was in November 1826, four months before his death. In truth this gaiety is not of the usual kind; for at times it is the harsh and spasmodic laughter of which Mocheles speaks; often it is the affecting smile, the result of suffering con quered. It matters not; he is the conqueror. He does not believe in death.

It came, however. At the end of November, 1826, he caught a chill which turned to pleurisy : he was taken ill in Vienna when returning from a journey undertaken in winter to arrange for the future of his nephew.[3] He was far from his friends.

---

[1] In 1819 he was followed by the police for having said aloud " That, after all, Christ was only a crucified Jew." He was then writing the *Mass in D*. That work alone is enough to show the freedom of his religious inspirations. (For the religious opinions of Beethoven, see Theodor von Frimmel ; *Beethoven,* 3rd Edition, Verlag Harmonie ; and *Beethovenia,* edited by Georg Müller, Vol. 11, Blöchinger). No less free in politics, Beethoven boldly attacked the vices of the government. He attacked amongst other things, the administration of justice, hindered by the slowness of its process, the stupid police regulations, the rude and lazy clerks in office, who killed all individual initiative and paralysed all action : the unfair privileges of a degenerative aristocracy, the high taxation, etc. His political sympathies seemed to be with England at that time.

[2] The suicide of his nephew.

[3] See an article by Dr. Klotz Forest on the last illness and

He told his nephew to go for a doctor. The wretch forgot his commission and only remembered two days after. The doctor came too late and treated Beethoven unskilfully. For three months his iron constitution fought against the illness. On January 3rd, 1827, he made his well-loved nephew his chief executor. He thought of his dear friends on the Rhine; he wrote again to Wegeler : " How I would like to talk with you ! But I am too weak. I can do no more than embrace you in my heart, you and your Lorchen." Poverty would have made his last moments more gloomy, had it not been for the generosity of some English friends. He had become very gentle and very patient.[1] On his death-bed on February 17th, 1827, after three operations and awaiting a fourth,[2] he wrote with perfect calmness, " I am patient and I think that all misfortune brings some blessing with it." This boon was deliverance—" the end of the comedy," as he said when dying. We might say rather the end of the *tragedy*. . . . . . He died in the climax of a violent storm, a tempest of snow, heavily punctuated with terrible thunder

death of Beethoven in the *Chronique Médicale* of April 1st and 15th, 1906. There is also exact information in the conversation books where the doctor's questions are written down, and in the article of the doctor himself (Dr. Wawruch) in the *Vienna Times*, in 1842.

1 The recollections of the singer, Ludwig Cramolini, which have been published, relate a touching visit to Beethoven during his last illness. He found Beethoven possessed of a calm serenity, a touching kindness. (See the *Frankfurter Zeitung*, of September 29th, 1907).

2 The operations took place on December 20th, January 8th, February 2nd, and February 27th.

claps. A strange hand closed his eyes,[1] March 26th, 1827.

. . . . . .

Beloved Beethoven! So many others have praised his artistic grandeur. But he is easily the first of musicians. He is the most heroic soul in modern art. He is the grandest and the best friend of those who suffer and struggle. When we are saddened by worldly miseries, it is he who comes near to us, as he used to go and play to a mother in grief, and without uttering a word thus console her by the song of his own plaintive resignation. And when we are utterly exhausted in the eternal battle uselessly waged against mediocrity, vice and virtue, it is an unspeakable boon to find fresh strength in this great ocean-torrent of strong will and faith. An atmosphere of courage emanates from his personality, a love of battle,[2] the exultation of a conscious

1 The young musician, Anselm Huttenbrenner. " God be praised," said Breuning. " Let us thank Him for having put an end to this long and pitiful martyrdom."

All Beethoven's MSS. books and furniture were sold by auction for 1,575 florins. The catalogue contained 252 lots of manuscripts and musical books which did not exceed the sum of 982 florins 37 kreutzer. The *conversation-books* and the *Tagebucher* were sold for 1 florin 20 kreutzer. Amongst his books Beethoven possessed: Kant's *Natural Science and Astronomy;* Bode'-*Knowledge of the Heavens;* Thomas à Kempis *The Imitation of Christ.* The Censor confiscated Seum's *Walks round Syracuse* Kotzebue's *Over the Adel,* and Fessler's *Views on Religion and Theology.*

2 "I am always happy when I have to master some difficulty" (Letter to the Immortal Loved One). " I should like to live a thousand lives. . . I am not suited for a quiet life." (To Wegeler, November 16th, 1801).

feeling of the *God within*. It seems that in his constant communion with nature[1] he had ended by assimilating its deep and mighty powers. Grillparzer, who admired Beethoven with a kind of awe, said of him, " He penetrated into regions where art melts away and unites with the wild and capricious elements." Schumann wrote similarly of his *Symphony in C minor*: " Every time it is performed it exercises an unvarying power on us, like natural phenomena which fill us with awe and amazement every time they occur." And Schindler, his confidential friend, says, " He possessed the spirit of nature." It is true, " Beethoven is a force of nature; and this battle of elemental power against the rest of nature is a spectacle of truly Homeric grandeur."

His whole life is like a stormy day. At the beginning—a fresh clear morning, perhaps a languid breeze, scarcely a breath of air. But there is already in the still air a secret menace, a dark foreboding. Large shadows loom and pass; tragic rumblings; murmuring awesome silences; the furious gusts of the winds of the *Eroica* and the *C minor*. However, the freshness of the day is not yet gone. Joy remains joy; the brightness of the sky is not overcast; sadness is never without a ray of hope. But after 1810 the poise of the

1 " Beethoven talked to me on the science of nature and helped me with this study as with music. It was not the laws of nature but its elementary powers that attracted him." (Schindler).

soul is disturbed. A strange light glows. Mists obscure his deepest thoughts; some of the clearer thoughts appear as vapour rising; they disappear, are dispelled, yet form anew; they obscure the heart with their melancholy and capricious gloom; often the musical idea seems to vanish entirely, to be submerged, but only to re-appear again at the end of a piece in a veritable storm of melody. Even joy has assumed a rough and riotous character. A bitter feeling becomes mingled in all his sentiments.[1] Storms gather as evening comes on. Heavy clouds are big with tempests. Lightning flashes o'er the black of night. The climax of the hurricane is approaching. Suddenly, at the height of the tempest, the darkness is dispersed. Night is driven away and the clear, tranquil atmosphere is restored by a sheer act of will power. What a conquest was this! What Napoleonic battle can be likened to it? What was Austerlitz glory to the radiance of this superhuman effort, this victory, the most brilliant that has ever been won by an infirm and lonely spirit. Sorrow personified, to whom the world refused joy, created joy himself to give to the world. He forged it from his own misery, as he proudly said in reviewing his life. And indeed it was the motto of his whole heroic soul:

JOY THROUGH SUFFERING
(To Countess Erdödy, October 19th, 1815).

.   .   .   .   .   .

1 " Oh, how good life is; but mine is for ever embittered." (Letter to Wegeler, May 2nd, 1810).

HIS WILL

Adagio

A - lone,   A - lone,   A - lone.

(To Lichnovsky, 21 Sept., 1814).

THE HEILIGENSTADT WILL.[1]

For my brothers CARL and —— BEETHOVEN.

O ye men who regard or declare me to be
malignant, stubborn or cynical, how unjust are
ye towards me! You do not know the secret cause
of my seeming so. From childhood onward, my
heart and mind prompted me to be kind and tender,
and I was ever inclined to accomplish great deeds.
But only think that during the last six years I
have been in a wretched condition, rendered worse
by unintelligent physicians. Deceived from year
to year with hopes of improvement, and then
finally forced to the prospect of *lasting infirmity*
(which may last for years, or even be totally incurable). Born with a fiery, active temperament,
even susceptive of the diversions of society, I had
soon to retire from the world, to live a solitary life.
At times, even, I endeavoured to forget all this,
but how harshly was I driven back by the redoubled
experience of my bad hearing. Yet it was not
possible for me to say to men: "Speak louder,
shout, for I am deaf." Alas! how could I declare

1 Translation by J. S. Shedlock. See footnote, page 65.

57

the weakness of a *sense* which in me *ought to be*
more acute than in others—a sense which *formerly*
I possessed in highest perfection, a perfection such
as few in my profession enjoy, or ever have enjoyed; no, I cannot do it. Forgive, therefore, if
you see me withdraw, when I would willingly mix
with you. My misfortune pains me doubly, in that
I am certain to be misunderstood. For me there
can be no recreation in the society of my fellow
creatures, no refined conversations, no interchange
of thought. Almost alone, and only mixing in
society when absolutely necessary, I am compelled
to live as an exile. If I approach near to people,
a feeling of hot anxiety comes over me lest my
condition should be noticed—for so it was during
these past six months which I spent in the country.
Ordered by my intelligent physician to spare my
hearing as much as possible, he almost fell in with
my present frame of mind, although many a time
I was carried away by my sociable inclinations.
But how humiliating was it, when some one
standing close to me heard a distant flute, and I
heard *nothing,* or a *shepherd singing,* and again
I heard nothing. Such incidents almost drove me
to despair; at times I was on the point of putting
an end to my life—*art* alone restrained my hand.
Oh! it seemed as if I could not quit this earth
until I had produced all I felt within me, and so
I continued this wretched life, wretched indeed,
with so sensitive a body that a somewhat sudden
change can throw me from the best into the worst

state. *Patience,* I am told, I must choose as my guide. I have done so—lasting, I hope, will be my resolution to bear up until it pleases the inexorable Parcae to break the thread. Forced, already in my 28th year,[1] to become a philosopher it is not easy; for an artist more difficult than for any one else. O Divine Being, Thou Who lookest down into my inmost soul, Thou understandest, Thou knowest that love for mankind and a desire to do good dwell therein. Oh, my fellow men, when one day you read this, remember that you were unjust to me, and let the unfortunate one console himself if he can find one like himself, who in spite of all obstacles which nature has thrown in his way, has still done everything in his power to be received into the ranks of worthy artists and men. You, my brothers Carl and ——, as soon as I am dead, beg Professor Schmidt, if he be still living, to describe my malady, and annex this written account to that of my illness, so that at least the world may know, so far as it is possible, may become reconciled to me after my death. And now I declare you both heirs to my small fortune (if such it may be called). Divide it honourably and dwell in peace, and help each other. What you have done against me, has, as you know, long been forgiven. And you, brother Carl, I especially thank you for the attachment you have shown towards me of late. My prayer is that your

1 Beethoven was at the time in his 32nd year; but he never knew precisely his age.

life may be better, less troubled by cares than mine. Recommend to your children virtue; it alone can bring happiness, not money.   I speak from experience. It was virtue which bore me up in time of trouble; to her, next to my art, I owe thanks for my not having laid violent hands on myself. Farewell, and love one another. My thanks to all friends, especially *Prince Lichnovsky and Professor Schmidt.* I should much like one of you to keep as an heirloom the instruments given to me by Prince L., but let no strife arise between you concerning them; if money should be of more service to you, just sell them. How happy I feel that even when lying in my grave I may be useful to you.

So let it be. I joyfully hasten to meet death. If it come before I have had opportunity to develop all my artistic faculties, it will come, my hard fate notwithstanding, too soon, and I should probably wish it later—yet even then I shall be happy, for will it not deliver me from a state of endless suffering?   Come when thou wilt, I shall face thee courageously; farewell, and when I am dead, do not entirely forget me. This I deserve from you, for during my lifetime I often thought of you, and how to make you happy. Be ye so.

LUDWIG VAN BEETHOVEN.

Heiglnstadt, the 6th of October, 1802.

(Black Seal).

On the fourth side of the large Will sheet :—

Heiglnstadt, October, 1802, thus I take my farewell of thee—and, indeed, sadly—yes, that fond hope which I entertained when I came here, of being at any rate healed up to a certain point, must be entirely abandoned. . As the leaves of autumn fall and fade, so it has withered away for me; almost the same as when I came here do I go away—even the high courage which often in the beautiful summer days quickened me, that has vanished. O Providence, let me have just one pure day of *joy;* so long is it since true joy filled my heart. Oh when, oh when, oh Divine Being, shall I be able once again to feel it in the temple of nature and of men ? Never—no—that would be too hard.

For my brothers Carl and ——— to execute after my death.

CODICIL. TESTAMENTARY DISPOSITION.

My nephew, Carl, shall be my sole heir; the capital of my estate shall, however, descend to his natural heirs or to those appointed by him through a will.

Ludwig van Beethoven.

LETTERS

BEETHOVEN
AT THE AGE OF 44.

*(From an Engraving by Blasius Hoefel after the
Drawing by Louis Letronne, 1814*

[To face page 64.

BEETHOVEN'S LETTERS.*

I.

To CARL AMENDA at Wirben in Courland.

(*Vienna, June* 1, 1800).
My dear, my good Amenda, my heartily beloved
friend.

With deep emotion, with mixed pain and
pleasure did I receive and read your last letter.
To what can I compare your fidelity, your attachment to me. Oh! how pleasant it is that
you have always remained so kind to me; yes,
I also know that you, of all men, are the most
trustworthy. You are no *Viennese friend;* no,
you are one of those such as my native country
produces. How often do I wish you were with
me, your Beethoven is most unhappy, and at
strife with nature and Creator. The latter I have
often cursed for exposing His creatures to the
smallest chance, so that frequently the richest
buds are thereby crushed and destroyed. Only

---

* For the Letters, I have been kindly allowed by Messrs. J.
M. Dent & Co., to use Mr. J. S. Shedlock's splendid translation
in his monumental, " *Letters of Ludwig van Beethoven* " (2
volumes, 1909), which contain no less than 7,220 documents.

think that the noblest part of me, my sense of
hearing has become very weak. Already, when
you were with me I noticed traces of it, and I
said nothing. Now it has become worse, and
it remains to be seen whether it can ever be
healed. . . . . I much fear that my hearing will not
improve; maladies of that kind are the most
difficult of all to cure. What a sad life I am
now compelled to lead; I must avoid all that is
near and dear to me, and then to be among
such wretched egotistical beings such as . . . . .
etc. I can say that among all, Lichnowski has
best stood the test. Since last year he has settled
on me 600 florins, which, together with the good
sale of my works, enables me to live without
anxiety. Everything I write I can sell immediately five times over, and also be well paid.
I have composed a fair quantity, and as I hear
you have ordered pianofortes from . . . I will send
you many things in one of the packing cases so
it will not cost you so very much. Now to my
consolation, a man has come here with whom
intercourse is a pleasure, and whose friendship
is free from all selfishness. He is one of the
friends of my youth. I have often spoken to
him about you, and told him that since I left my
native country, you are the one whom my heart
has chosen. Even he does not like . . . . . the
latter is and remains too weak for friendship.
I consider him and . . . . . . mere instruments
on which when it pleases me I play; but they

can never become noble witnesses of my inner and outer activity, nor be in true sympathy with me; I value them according as they are useful to me. Oh! how happy should I now be if I had my perfect hearing, for I should then hasten to you. As it is, I must in all things be behindhand; my best years will slip away without bringing forth what, with my talent and my strength I ought to have accomplished. I must now have recourse to sad resignation. I have, it is true, resolved not to worry about all this but how is it possible? Yes, Amenda, if six months hence my malady is beyond cure, then I lay claim to your help. You must leave everything and come to me. I will travel (my malady interferes least with my playing and composition, most only in conversation), and you must be my companion. I am convinced good fortune will not fail me. With whom need I be afraid of measuring my strength? Since you went away I have written music of all kinds except operas and sacred works.

Yes, do not refuse; help your friend to bear with his troubles, his infirmity. I have also greatly improved my pianoforte playing. I hope this journey may also turn to your advantage; afterwards you will always remain with me. I have duly received all your letters, and although I have only answered a few, you have been always in my mind, and my heart, as always, beats tenderly for you. *Please keep as a great secret*

*what I have told you about my hearing; trust
no one, whoever it may be, with it.* Do write
frequently; your letters, however short they may
be, console me, do me good. I expect soon to
get another one from you, my dear friend. Don't
lend out my Quartet any more, because I have
made many changes in it. I have only just learnt
how to write quartets properly, as you will see
when you receive them.

Now, my dear good friend, farewell! If,
perchance, you believe that I can show you any
kindness here, I need not of course, remind you
to first address yourself to

Your faithful, truly loving,

L. v. BEETHOVEN.

II.

To Fraulein GERARDI.

Dear Chr.   (1798?)

You let me hear something yesterday about
a portrait of myself. I wish you to proceed
somewhat carefully in the matter. I fear if we
return it through F., the disagreeable B. or the
arch-fool Joseph might interfere, and then the
matter might be meant as a mean trick played
on me, and that would be really most annoying.
I should have to avenge myself, and the whole
populasse does not deserve it. Try to get hold
of the thing as well as you can. I assure you
that after this I should put a notice in the news-

paper, requesting all painters not to take my portrait without my consent, were I afraid of falling into perplexity over my own countenance. As to the matter of taking off my hat, it is altogether stupid, and at the same time too impolite for me to retaliate. Pray explain to him the truth about the walk.

Adieu. The devil take you.

III.

To Frl. ÉLEONORE VON BREUNING in Bonn.

Vienna, November 2, 1793.

Honoured Eleonore, my dearest friend.

I shall soon have been in this capital a whole year, yet only now do you receive a letter from me, but you were certainly constantly in my thoughts. Frequently, indeed, did I hold converse with you and your dear family, but, for the most part, not with the tranquility of mind which I should have liked. Then it was that the fatal quarrel hovered before me, and my former behaviour appeared to me so abominable. But the past cannot be undone, and what would I not give if I could blot out of my life my former conduct so dishonouring to me, so contrary to my character. Many circumstances, indeed, kept us at a distance from each other, and, as I presume, it was especially the insinuations resulting from conversations on either side which prevented all reconciliation. Each of us believed that he was convinced of the truth of what he said, and yet it was mere anger, and we were both deceived. Your good and noble character is, indeed, a guarantee that I have long since been forgiven. But true repentance consists, so it is said, in acknowledging one's faults, and this I intended to do. And now let us draw a curtain over the whole story, and only learn from it the lesson that when friends fall out it is always better to have no go-between, but for friend to turn directly to friend.

Herewith you receive a dedication from me to yourself, and I only wish that the work were more important, more worthy of you. I have been worried here to publish this small work,[1] and I make use of this opportunity to give you, my adorable Eleonore, a proof of my high esteem and of my friendship towards you, and of my constant remembrance of your family. Accept this trifle, and realise that it comes from a friend who holds you in high esteem. Oh, if it only gives you pleasure, I am fully rewarded. Let it be a small re-awakening of that time in which I spent so many and such happy hours in your home; it may, perhaps, keep me in your remembrance, until one day I return, but that will not be for a long time. Oh, how we shall then rejoice, my dear

[1] The variations mentioned were those for Piano and Violin on the well-known theme, *Se vuol ballar,* from Mozart's *Figaro.* (See page 226, 1A).

friend. You will then find your friend a more cheerful being, for whom time and his better fortune have smoothed down the furrows of the horrid past. If you happen to see B. Koch, please tell her that it is not nice of her not to have sent me a single line. For I have written twice; to Malchus I wrote three times—and no answer. Tell her that if she would not write, she ought to have urged Malchus to do so. As conclusion to my letter, I add a request; it is that I may be lucky enough, my dear friend, again to possess an Angola vest knitted by your hands. Forgive this indiscreet request from your friend. It arises from the great preference I have for everything coming from your hands, and, as a secret, I may say to you that in this there is at bottom a little vanity, viz., to be able to say that I possess something given to me by one of the best, most worthy young ladies in Bonn. I still have the first one which you were kind enough to give me in Bonn, but it is now so out of fashion that I can only keep it in my wardrobe as a precious gift from you. If you would soon write me a nice letter, it would afford me great pleasure. If, perchance, my letters give you pleasure, I certainly promise that I will willingly send news as often as I can. For everything is welcome to me whereby I can show you in what esteem you are held by

Your true friend,

L. v. BEETHOVEN.

IV.

To Dr. F. WEGELER in Bonn.

Vienna, June 29, 1800.

My good, dear Wegeler.

I am most grateful to you for thinking of me; I have so little deserved it, or sought to deserve it at your hands. And yet you are so very good, and are not kept back by anything, not even by my unpardonable negligence, but always remain a faithful, good, honest friend. That I could ever forget you, and especially all of you who were so kind and affectionate to me, no, do not believe it; there are moments in which I myself long for you—yes, and wish to spend some time with you. My native land, the beautiful country in which I first saw the light of the world, is ever as beautiful and distinct before mine eyes as when I left you. In short, I shall regard that time as one of the happiest of my life, when I see you again, and can greet our father Rhine. When that will be I cannot yet say. This much will I tell you, that you will only see me again when I am really great; not only greater as an artist, but as a man you shall find me better, more perfect; and if in our native land there are any signs of returning prosperity, I will only use my art for the benefit of the poor. O, happy moment, how fortunate I think myself in being able to get a fatherland created here!

You want to know something about my present state; well, at present, it is not so bad. Since last year, Lichnowsky, who, however incredible it may seem when I tell it you, was always my warmest friend, and has remained so (of course, there have been slight misunderstandings between us, but just these have strengthened our friendship), has settled a fixed sum of 600 florins on me, and I can draw it so long as I fail to find a suitable post. My compositions are bringing in a goodly sum, and I may add, it is scarcely possible for me to execute the orders given. Also, for every work I have six, seven publishers, and if I choose, even more. They do not bargain with me; I demand and they pay. You see how pleasant it is. For example, I see a friend in distress, and if my purse do not allow of my helping him, I have only to sit down and in a short time he is relieved. Also I am more economical than I was formerly. If I should settle here, I shall certainly contrive to get one day every year for concerts, of which I have given some.

Only my envious demon, my bad health, has thrown obstacles in my way. For instance, my hearing has become weaker during the last three years, and this infirmity was in the first instance caused by my general health, which, as you know, was already, in the past, in a wretched state. Frank wished to restore me to health by means of strengthening medicines, and to cure my deafness by means of oil of almonds, but, *prosit!* nothing came of these remedies; my hearing became worse and worse, and my ill-health always remained in its first state. This continued until the autumn of last year, and ofttimes I was in despair. Then an Asinus of a doctor advised cold baths; a more skilful one, the usual tepid Danube baths. These worked wonders; the state of my health improved, my deafness remained, or became worse. This winter I was truly miserable. I had terrible attacks of colic, and I fell quite back into my former state. So I remained for about four weeks and then went to Vering, for I thought that this state required medical aid, and in addition I had always placed faith in him. He ordered tepid Danube baths, and whenever I took one I had to pour into it a little bottle full of strengthening stuff. He gave me no medicine until about four days ago, when he ordered an application of herbs for the ear. And through these I can say I feel stronger and better; only the humming in my ears continues day and night without ceasing. I may truly say that my life is a wretched one. For the last two years I have avoided all society, for it is impossible for me to say to people ' I am deaf.' Were my profession any other it would not so much matter, but in my profession it is a terrible thing; and my enemies, of whom they are not a few, what would they say to this? To give you an idea of this extraordinary deafness, I will tell you that when at the theatre, I am obliged to lean forward close to the orchestra, in order to understand what is being said on the stage. When somewhat at a distance I cannot hear the high tones of instruments, voices. In speaking it is not surprising that there are people who have never noticed it, for as a rule I am absent-minded, and they account for it in that way. Often I can scarcely hear anyone speaking to me; the tones, yes, but not the actual words; yet as soon as anyone shouts, it is unbearable. What will come of all this, heaven only knows! Vering says that there will *certainly be an improvement, though perhaps not a perfect cure.* I have, indeed, often ———— ———— cursed my existence; Plutarch taught r·· resignation. If nothing else is possible I will defy my fate, although there will be moments in my life when I shall be God's most wretched creature. I beg you not to tell anyone about this; don't say even a word to Lorchen. I only tell it you as a secret; I should be glad if you would open up correspondence with Vering on the subject. Should my present state continue, I would come next spring to you. You would take a house for me in some beautiful place in the country, and so I would rusticate for six months. By that means there might come a change. Resignation! what a miserable refuge, and yet it is the only way for me.

Pray forgive me for telling you of a friend's

trouble, when you yourself are in sad circumstances. Stephen Breuning is now here, and we
are together almost daily. It does me good to
hark back to old times. He is really a good, noble
young fellow, who knows a thing or two, and
whose heart, as with all of us more or less, is
sound. I have very fine rooms now, which look
on to the bastion, and this for my health is of
double value. I really think I can arrange for
Breuning to come and live with me. You shall
have your Antiochus, and a rare lot of my new
compositions, unless you think it will cost you
too much. Honestly speaking, your love for art
gives me the highest pleasure. Only write to me
how it is to be managed, and I will send you
all my works, of which the number is now pretty
large and it is daily increasing. In place of the
portrait of my grandfather, which I beg you to
send as soon as possible by stage coach, I send
you that of his grandson, your ever good and
affectionate Beethoven. It is coming out here at
Artaria's, who, also other art firms, have often
asked me for it. I will write shortly to Stoffel,
and read him a bit of a lecture about his cross
temper. He shall hear what I have to say about
old friendship, he shall promise on his oath not
to grieve you any more in your, apart from this,
sad circumstances. I will also write to kind
Lorchen. I have never forgot a single one of
you, my dear good people, although you never
get any news from me; but writing, as you well

know, was never a strong point with me—years, even, have passed without my best friends ever receiving anything. I only live in my music, and I have scarcely begun one thing when I start another. As I am now working, I am often engaged on three or four things at the same time.

Write often to me now; I will see to it that I find time sometimes to write to you. Greetings to all, also to the good wife of the privy councillor, and tell her that I still, occasionally, have a "raptus." I am not surprised at the change in K; fortune is fickle, and does not always fall to the most worthy, the best. A word about Ries, to whom hearty greetings. As regards his son, about whom I will write shortly, although I am of opinion that to make his way in the world, Paris is better than Vienna. The latter city is overcrowded, and even persons of the highest merit find it hard to maintain themselves. By the autumn, or the winter, I will see what I can do for him, for then every one is returning.

Farewell, good, faithful Wegeler. Rest assured of the love and friendship of

Your,
BEETHOVEN.

V.

To Dr. FRANZ WEGELER in Bonn.

November 16 (1801 ?)

My good Wegeler.

I thank you for the fresh proof of your anxiety concerning myself, and all the more as I am so little deserving of it. You want to know how I am, what I am taking; and however unwillingly I may discuss the matter, I certainly like best to do it with you. For the last few months, Vering has ordered herb plasters to be constantly placed on both arms; and these, as you will know, are composed of a certain bark. This is a most unpleasant cure, as, until the bark has sufficiently drawn, I am deprived for a day or so of the free use of my arms, to say nothing of the pain. I cannot, it is true, deny that the humming with which my deafness actually began, has become somewhat weaker, especially in the left ear. My hearing, however, has not in the least improved; I really am not quite sure whether it has not become worse. My general health is better, and especially after I have taken luke warm baths a few times, I am fairly well for eight or ten days. I seldom take any tonic; I am now applying herb-plasters according to your advice. Vering won't hear of shower baths, but I am really very dissatisfied with him; he shows so little care and forbearance for such a malady, if I did not actually go to him, and that costs me a great effort, I should never see him. What is your opinion of Schmidt? I do not like making a change, yet it seems to me that Vering is too much a practitioner to be able to take in new ideas through books. Schmidt appears to me a very different kind of man, and perhaps would not be so remiss. I hear wonders of galvanism; what do you say about it? A doctor told me he had seen a deaf and dumb child in Berlin who had recovered his hearing, also a man who had been deaf for seven years. I have just heard that your Schmidt is making experiments with it.

My life is again somewhat pleasanter, for I mix in society. You can scarcely imagine what a dreary, sad life I have led during the past two years. My weak hearing always seemed to me like a ghost and I ran away from people, was forced to appear a misanthrope, though not at all in my character. This change has been brought about by an enchanting maiden, who loves me, and whom I love. Again during the past two years I have had some happy moments, and for the first time I feel that marriage can bring happiness. Unfortunately, she is not of my station in life, and now—for the moment I certainly could not marry—I must bravely bustle about. If it were not for my hearing, I should already long ago have travelled half over the world, and that I must do. For me there is no greater pleasure than that of practising and displaying my art. Do not believe that I should feel happy among you. What, indeed, could make me happier? Even your solicitude would pain me; at every moment I should read pity on your faces, and that would make me still more miserable. My beautiful native country, what was my lot when there? Nothing but hope of a better state, and, except for this evil, I should already have won it! O that I could be free from it, and encompass the world! My youth, yes I feel it, is only now beginning; have I not always been sickly? My strength, both of body and mind, for some time has been on the increase. Every day I approach nearer to the goal; this I feel, though I can scarcely describe it. Only through this, can your Beethoven live. Don't talk of rest! I know no other but sleep, and sorry enough am I, that I am compelled to give more time to it than formerly. If only half freed from my infirmity, then—as a thorough, ripe man—I will come to you and renew the old feelings of friendship. You will see me as happy as my lot can be here below, not unhappy. No, that I could not endure; I will seize fate by the throat; it shall certainly never wholly overcome me. Oh! life is so beautiful, would I could have a thousand lives! I feel I am no longer fit to lead a quiet life! Do write as soon as you can. See to it that Stephen makes up his mind to get an appointment in the Order of German Knights.

For his health, life here is too fatiguing. And besides, he leads such a retired life, that I do not see how he can get on. You know how it is here; I do not mean to say that society would render him less languid; he can never be persuaded to go into it. Some time ago I had a musical party at my house; but our friend Stephen did not turn up. Do advise him to take more rest and to be more steady. I have done all I could; without he takes this advice, he can never become either happy or healthy. Now, tell me in your next letter, whether it matters if I send you a· great deal of my music. What you really don't want you can sell, and so you will have your postage—also my portrait. Best remembrances to Lorchen—also Mamma—and Christoph. You do really love me a little, do you not? Be as well assured of this (of my love), as of the friendship of your

BEETHOVEN.

VI.

To CAPELLMEISTER HOFMEISTER in Leipzig.

Vienna, 15*th* (or something like it),
January, 1801.
With great pleasure, my dearly beloved brother and friend, have I read your letter. I thank you right heartily for the good opinion you have expressed concerning me and my works,

G

and hope I may prove myself really worthy of
it. Please also convey my dutiful thanks to
Herr K. for his courtesy and friendly feelings
towards me.

Your undertakings likewise make me glad,
and I hope, if works of art can procure gain,
that it will fall to the lot of genuine true artists,
rather than to mere shopkeepers. That you wish
to publish the works of *Sebastian* Bach rejoices
my heart, which beats in unison with the high
art of this forefather of harmony, and I desire
soon to see the scheme in full swing. I hope
that here, so soon as golden peace has been pro-
claimed, I shall be able to be of great assistance
in the matter, when you issue a subscription
list. As regards our special business, since you
wish it, I hope this may be to your liking: I
now offer you the following : *Septet* (concerning
which I have already written to you ; by *arrang-
ing* it for pianoforte, it would become better
known and be more profitable) 20 ducats, *Symphony* 20 ducats, *Concerto* 10 ducats, *Solo
Sonata (Allegro, Adagio, Minuetto, Rondo)* 20
ducats.   This *Sonata* is A1, dearest brother !
Now for a word of explanation; you will perhaps
be surprised that I here make no difference between *Sonata, Septet, Symphony,* because I find
that there is not such a demand for a Septet or
a *Symphony* as for a Sonata ; that is why I do so,
although a *Symphony* is undoubtedly of greater
value (N.B.—the Septet consists of a short

introductory *Adagio*, then *Allegro*, *Adagio*, *Minuetto*, *Andante* with *Variations*, *Minuetto*, another short introductory *Adagio*, and then *Presto*). The *Concerto* I only value at 10 ducats, because, as I have already written, I do not give it out as one of my best. All things considered, I do not think you will find this excessive; anyhow I have tried to name prices for you as moderate as I possibly could. Concerning the money order, since you leave me the choice, you could make it payable at Geimüller's or Schüller's. The full amount would therefore be 70 ducats for all four works. I do not understand any other money than Viennese ducats; how many thalers and gulden that makes, is no affair of mine, for I am a bad *business* man and reckoner.

There is an end of the troublesome business. So I name it, because I only wish it could be otherwise in the world. There ought to be an artistic *depôt* where the artist need only hand in his art-work in order to receive what he asks for. As things are, one must be half a business man, and how can one understand,—good heavens!— that's what I really call *troublesome*. As for the Leipzig O (?) let them just go on talking; *they* will never by their chatter confer immortality on any one, neither can they take it away from any one for whom Apollo has destined it. Now, may heaven have *you and yours* in its keeping. For some time I have not been well; and so it is now somewhat difficult for me to write notes,

still more so alphabet letters. I hope that we
shall often have opportunity to assure ourselves
that you are a great friend to me, and that I am
  Your devoted
    brother and friend,
       L. v. BEETHOVEN.

VII.

Letter from Wegeler and Eleonore von Breuning
    to Beethoven.

    Coblentz, 28 December, 1825.
My dear old Louis.
  I cannot allow one of Ries' ten children
to leave Vienna without recalling him to your
remembrance. If during the twenty-eight years
since I left Vienna, you have not received a
long letter from me every two months, you must
put it down to your own silence after the first
letters which I sent you. It should not be so
and especially now that we other old people
live so entirely in the past and derive our chief
pleasure in recollections of our youth. For me
at least, my acquaintance and my firm friendship
to you, thanks to your good mother whom God
now blesses, is a guiding star in my life, towards which I turn with pleasure. . . . I raise
my eyes to you as to a hero, and I am proud to
be able to say : ' I have had some influence on
his development; he confided in me his ambitions

and his dreams; and when later he was so often misunderstood, I knew quite well what he wanted.' God be praised that I have been able to speak of you with my wife, and now with my children! My mother-in-law's house was more your home than your own home, especially after the death of your good mother. Tell us still once more, ' I think of you both in joy and in sorrow.' A man, even when he has risen as high as you, is only happy once in his life : when he is young. Your thoughts should hark back happily many times to the stones of Bonn, Godesburg, Pépinière, etc. Now I want to speak of myself, of ourselves, to give you an example of how you ought to reply to me.

After my return from Vienna in 1796, things went rather badly with me. For a long time I had to rely for a living on my consultations as a doctor, and that lasted for several years in this wretched country, before I could even make a bare livelihood. Then I became a professor with a salary, and I married. A year later I had a daughter who is still living and who is quite accomplished. In addition to a very clear head, she has the quiet ways of her father; and she plays admirably some of Beethoven's Sonatas. She can claim no merit for this, for it is an inborn gift with her. In 1807 I had a son who is now studying medicine in Berlin. In four years I shall send him to Vienna. Will you look after him for me ? I celebrated, in August, my 60th birthday by a party of sixty friends and acquaintances, including the chief people of Bonn. I have lived here since 1807, and have a fine house and a good position. My superiors are satisfied with me, and the King has given me some orders and medals. Lore and I are content. Now that I have told you all about ourselves, it is your turn. . . .

Do you never wish to turn your eyes from the tower of St. Stephen's? Has travel no charms for you? Do you never wish to see the Rhine again? With every good wish from Madam Lore and myself,

Your very old friend,

WEGELER.

Coblentz, 29 December, 1825.

Dear Beethoven—dear for such a long time!

It was my wish that Wegeler should write to you again. Now that this is done, I should like to add a few words—not only to recall myself to your remembrance, but to renew the pressing question whether you have not a desire to see the Rhine and your birthplace again, and to give Wegeler and me the greatest joy possible. Our Lenchen thanks you for so many happy hours; she delights in hearing us speak of you; she knows all the little adventures of our happy youthful days at Bonn—of the quarrel and the reconciliation. . . . How happy she would be to see you! Unfortunately, the little one has no special aptitude for music; but she has done so much by application and perseverance that she can play your Sonatas, Variations, etc.; and as music is always the greatest relaxation for Wegeler, she is thus able to give him many happy hours. Julius has some talent for music, but up to the present it has been neglected; for the last six months, he has been learning the violoncello with zest and pleasure; and as he has a good teacher in Berlin I believe that he will get on well. The two children are tall and resemble their father; they also possess that fine cheery disposition which Wegeler, thanks to God, has not even yet lost. . . . He takes great pleasure in playing the themes of your Variations; the old ones have the greater preference, but he oftens plays the new ones, too, with incredible patience. Your *Opferlied* is placed above everything. Wegeler never goes to his room without putting it on the piano. So, dear Beethoven, you can see how lasting and real a thing is the remembrance which we always have of you! Tell us then just once that this is not worthless to you, and that we are not quite forgotten. If it were not so difficult to do as one wishes, we should already have been to Vienna to see my brother, and have the pleasure of seeing you again; but such a journey is out of the question now that our son is at Berlin. Wegeler has told you how everything goes with us—we should do wrong to complain. Even the most difficult

times have been better for us than for hundreds
of others. The greatest blessing is that we all
keep well and that we have such good and noble
children. Yes, they have hardly given us any
trouble, and they are such merry and happy little
people. Lenchen has had only one great grief; it
was when our poor Burscheid died: a loss none
of us will ever forget. Adieu, dear Beethoven,
and think of us as the most loyal of friends.

ELN. WEGELER.

VIII.

To Dr. FRANZ WEGELER.
Vienna, 7th October, 1826.

My dear old friend.

　　I cannot tell you how much pleasure your
letter and that of your Lorchen gave me. Certainly, a reply ought to have been sent with
lightning speed, but I am generally somewhat
careless about writing, because I think that the
better sort of men know me without this. I
often compose the answer in my mind, but when
I wish to write it down, I usually throw the pen
away, because I cannot write as I feel. I remember all the love which you have constantly
shown me, for instance, when you had my room
whitewashed, and so pleasantly surprised me.
It is the same with the Breuning family. If
we were separated, that happened in the natural

course of things; every one must pursue and try
to attain distinction in his calling; but the eternal
unshaken foundations of virtue held us ever
firmly united. Unfortunately, I cannot write to
you to-day so much as I wished, as I am bed-
ridden, and therefore confine myself to answering
certain points of your letter.

You write that I am somewhere spoken of
as a natural son of the late King of Prussia;
I, likewise, heard of this long ago, but have made
it a principle never to write anything about myself, nor to reply to anything written about me.
So I willingly leave it to you to make known to
the world the uprightness of my parents, and
especially of my mother. You write about your
son. I need not say that if he comes here he
will find in me a friend and father, and if I
can help, or be of service to him in any way, I
will gladly do so.

I still have the silhouette of your Lorchen,
from which you will see that all the goodness
and affection shown to me in my youth are still
dear to me.

Of my diplomas, I will only tell you briefly,
that I am honorary member of the Royal Society
of Sciences of Sweden, as well as of Amsterdam,
and also honorary citizen of Vienna. A short
time ago a certain Dr. Spiker took with him my
last great Symphony with chorus to Berlin; it
is dedicated to the King, and I had to write the
dedication with my own hand. I had already

sought permission through the Embassy to be allowed to dedicate this work to the King, and it was granted. At Dr. Spiker's instigation, I was obliged myself to hand over to him the manuscript for the King, with the corrections in my own handwriting, as it was to be placed in the Royal Library. Something has been said to me about the red order of the Eagle, 2nd class; what will come of it, I do not know, for I have never sought such tokens of honour; yet in these times, they would not be unwelcome to me for many reasons.

Moreover, my motto is always: ' Nulla dies sine linea,' and if I ever let the Muse sleep, it is only that she may awaken all the stronger. I hope still to bring some great works into the world, and then, like an old child, to end my earthly career amongst good men.

You will also soon receive some music from Schott Brothers of Mainz. The portrait which you receive enclosed, is certainly an artistic masterpiece, but it is not the last which has been taken of me. With regard to tokens of honour, which I know will give you pleasure, I may also mention that a medal was sent to me by the late King of France with the inscription : ' Donné par le Roi à Monsieur Beethoven,'' accompanied by a very obliging letter from the premier gentilhomme du Roi Duc de Châtres.

My dear friend, for to-day, farewell. For the rest, the remembrance of the past takes hold of

me, and not without many tears will you receive
this letter. A beginning is now made, and you
will soon get another letter, and the more frequently you write, the more pleasure will you
give me. No inquiry is necessary on either side
concerning our friendship; and so, farewell. I
beg you to kiss and embrace your dear Lorchen
and the children in my name, and at the same
time to think of me. God be with you all.

As always, your true friend who honours
you,

BEETHOVEN.

IX.

To Dr. F. G. WEGELER in Bonn.

Vienna, February 17, 1827.

Fortunately I received your second letter
through Breuning. I am still too weak to
answer it, but you may believe me that everything in it is welcome and desirable. My re-
covery, if I may call it so, is very slow; a fourth
operation is to be expected, although the doctors
do not say anything about it. I am patiently
thinking that every evil has sometimes its good.
But now I am astonished to see from your last
letter that you have not received anything. From
the present letter you will perceive that I wrote
to you already on the tenth of December last
year. With the portrait, it is the same, as you
will see from the date when you receive it.

' Frau Steffen said,'[1] in short, Stephen wished
to send you these things if some opportunity
offered, but they remained lying here up to this
date; moreover until now, it was difficult to send
them back. You will now get the portrait by
post, through Schott and Co., who also send you
the music. I should like to tell you still much
more, but I am too weak, thus I can only embrace
you and your Lorchen in spirit.

With true friendship and affection to you
and yours, I am

Your old, true friend,

BEETHOVEN.

X.

To Sir G. SMART in London.

March 6, 1827.

I do not doubt that you, dear Sir, have
received through Herr Moscheles my letter of
the 22nd of February; but as I have found by
chance among my papers, S.'s address, I do not
hesitate to write direct to you and recall my request again to your mind.

Up to now I cannot look forward to an end
of my terrible illness; on the contrary, my sufferings, and with it, my cares, have still increased.
On the 29th of February I underwent my fourth
operation, and it may be, perhaps, my fate to
undergo a fifth or even more. If this continues,

---

1 Quotation from a well-known song.

my illness will surely last till the middle of summer, and what will then become of me? How
shall I then manage to live till I have recovered
strength enough to gain my own living by my
pen? In short, I will not trouble you further
with my complaints, and refer only to my letter
of the 22nd of February, asking you to use all
your influence to induce the Philharmonic
Society to carry out their former resolution
concerning the concert for my benefit.

XI.

To I. MOSCHELES in London.

Vienna, March 14, 1827.

My dear Moscheles.

Some days ago I found out through Herr
Lewinger that you inquired in a letter to him
of the 10th of February regarding the state of
my illness, of which so many different rumours
have been spread about. Although I have no
doubts whatever that my letter of the 24th of
February has arrived, which will explain everything you desire to know, I can but thank you
for your sympathy with my sad lot, and beseech
you to be solicitous about the request which you
know of from my first letter, and I am quite
convinced that, in union with Sir Smart and other
of my friends, you will succeed in bringing about
a favourable result for me at the Philharmonic

Society. I have once more written to Sir Smart about it.

On the 27th of February I underwent the fourth operation, and there are visible symptoms that I shall have to suffer a fifth. What does it tend to, and what will become of me if it continues for some time longer? A hard lot, indeed, has fallen upon me! However, I submit to the will of fate, and only pray to God so to ordain it in His divine will, that I may be protected from want as long as I have to endure death in life. This will give me strength to bear my lot, however terrible it may be, with humble submission to the will of the Most High.

Therefore, my dear Moscheles, I entrust once more my affair to you, and remain with greatest respect ever

Your friend,

L. van BEETHOVEN.

Hummel is here and has called on me several times.

XII.

To I. MOSCHELES in London.

Vienna, March 18, 1827.

With what emotion I read your letter of the 1st March is not to described in words. This magnanimity of the Philharmonic Society, with which they anticipated my request, has touched

my inmost heart. I, therefore, ask you, dear
Moscheles, to be the organ through which I can
express my most heartfelt thanks to the Philharmonic Society for their sympathy and help.
Tell these worthy men that if God restores me
to health, I shall try practically to show my
gratitude by works, and that I leave it to the
Society to choose what I shall write for them.
A whole sketched Symphony (the 10th) is in
my desk, also a new Overture, or even something else. As regards the concert which the
Philharmonic Society has resolved on giving for
my benefit, I beg the Society not to give up this
intention. In short, I shall try to fulfil any wish
expressed by the Society, and never have I
undertaken a work with such ardour as will now
be displayed. May it only please God to restore
me soon again to health, and then I shall prove
to these magnanimous Englishmen that I know
how to value their sympathy to me in my sad
condition.

I was compelled to accept the whole sum of
1,000 fl., since I was then in the disagreeable
position of having to draw out invested money.

Your noble behaviour I shall never forget,
and I shall soon render my thanks in particular
to Sir Smart and Herr Stump. The metronomised
Ninth Symphony please hand to the Philharmonic Society. Enclosed find the markings.

Your most devoted friend,

BEETHOVEN.

XIII.

SCHINDLER to B. SCHOTT SOHNE, Mainz.

Vienna, April 12, 1827.

I would already have liked to take the liberty of forwarding to you the enclosed document in the name of our Beethoven as his dying request; but after the passing away of our friend, there was so much business to attend to that I found it impossible. Unfortunately, it was not possible to get the document legalised, for that Beethoven would have had to sign it at the law court, which was utterly impossible. Beethoven, however, requested Court Councillor v. Breuning and myself to add our names as witnesses, as we were both present. We, therefore, believe that it will serve the purpose for which it was drawn up. I must further mention that in this document you possess the *last* signature of this immortal man; for this was the last stroke of his pen.

I cannot now refrain from telling you something about the last hours when he was still conscious (namely, on the 24th of March, from early morning until about one o'clock in the afternoon), for to you, sirs, this will surely be of great interest. When I came to him on the morning of the twenty-fourth of March, I found his face quite drawn; moreover, he was so weak that with the greatest effort he could only utter two or three intelligible words. The *Ordinarius* soon arrived, and, after watching him for a few moments, said to me: 'Beethoven's end is rapidly approaching.' As the business of the Will had been settled, so far as was possible, the previous day, there remained for us only one ardent wish: to get him reconciled with heaven, in order that the world might also be shown that he ended his life as a true Christian. The Professor Ordinarius wrote it down, and begged him in the name of all his friends, to partake of the Sacrament for the dying, where-upon he answered calmly and steadily: 'I will.' The doctor went away, leaving me to see to this. Beethoven then said to me: 'My only request is that you write to Schott and send him the document: he *will need it*. And write to him in my name, for I am too weak, and say that I much desire him to send the wine. Also, if you have still time to-day, write to England.' The clergyman came about twelve o'clock, and the religious ceremony took place in the most edifying manner. And now for the first time he seemed to feel that his end was approaching, for the clergyman had scarcely gone when he said to me and to young v. Breuning: '*Plaudite amici, comœdia finita est!*' Have I not al-ways said that it would be thus? He then, once again, begged me not to forget Schott; also again to write in his name to the Philharmonic

H

Society[1] to thank them for their great gift, and to add that the Society had comforted his last days, and that even on the brink of the grave he thanked the Society and the whole English nation for the great gift. God bless them.

At this moment the chancery servant of v. Breuning entered the room with the case of wine and the decoction, about quarter to one o'clock. I put the two bottles of Rüdesheimer and the two other bottles of the decoction on the table at his bedside. He looked at them, saying: ' 'Tis a pity, a pity, too late!' These were his last words. Immediately after, commenced the death throes, so that he could not utter a sound. Towards evening he lost consciousness and became delirious, which lasted up to the evening of the 25th, when visible signs of approaching death appeared. In spite of it, he died only on the 26th at quarter to six o'clock in the evening.

This death struggle was terrible to behold, for his constitution, especially his chest, was like that of a giant. Of your Rüdesheimer, he took still a few spoonfuls until he passed away.

Thus I have the pleasure of acquainting you with the last three days of our unforgettable friend.

In conclusion, accept the assurance, etc.,

ANTON SCHINDLER.

---

1 This English Society had sent him a present of £100 and a magnificent edition of Handel which gave him the greatest pleasure during his last days.

THOUGHTS

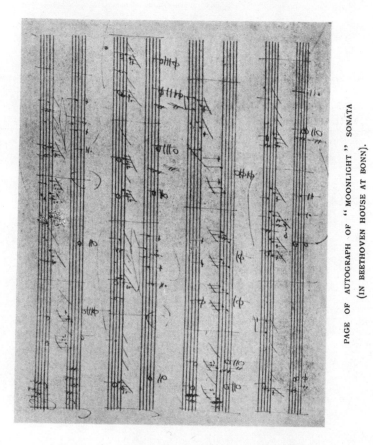

PAGE OF AUTOGRAPH OF "MOONLIGHT" SONATA
(IN BEETHOVEN HOUSE AT BONN).

[To face page 100.

THOUGHTS

ON MUSIC.

"*Il n'y a pas de règle qu'on ne peut blesser à cause de* SCHÖNER" (There is no rule which one cannot break for the sake of BEAUTY). This expression appears in the original in French except for the last word *Schöner*.

. . . . . .

" Music ought to create and fan the fire of the spirit of man."

. . . . . .

" Music is a higher revelation than the whole of wisdom and the whole of philosophy. . . . . He who penetrates the meaning of my music shall be freed from all the misery which afflicts others."

(To Bettina, 1810.)

. . . . . .

" There is nothing finer than to approach the Divine and to shed its rays on the human race."

. . . . . .

" Why do I write? What I have in my heart
must come out; and that is why I compose."

.　　.　　.　　.　　.　　.

" Do you believe that I think of a divine violin
when the spirit speaks to me and that I write what
it dictates?"

(To Schuppanzigh.)

.　　.　　.　　.　　.　　.

" According to my usual manner of composing,
even in my instrumental music, I always have the
whole in my mind; here, however, that whole is to
a certain extent divided; and I have afresh to think
myself into the music."

(To Treitschke: from correspondence concerning Beethoven's
musical settings to some of his poems. Treitschke was the
man who revised the libretto of *Fidelio* when it was seriously
thought of reviving it.)

.　　.　　.　　.　　.　　.

" One should compose without a piano. The
faculty of expressing what one desires and feels
(which is so essential a need to noble natures)
comes only by degrees."

(To the Archduke Rudolph.)

.　　.　　.　　.　　.　　.

" The descriptions of a picture belong to painting; even the poet in this matter may, in comparison with my art, esteem himself lucky, for his domain in this respect is not so limited as mine, yet the latter extends further into other regions, and to attain to our kingdom is not easy."

(To Wilhelm Gerhardi in Leipzig from Nussdorf, July, 1817.)

.   .   .   .   .   .

" Liberty and progress are the goals of art just as of life in general.   If we are not as solid as the old masters, the refinement of civilization has at least enlarged our outlook."

(To Archduke Rudolph.)

.   .   .   .   .   .

" I am not in the habit of altering my compositions when they are once finished.   I have never done this, for I hold firmly that the slightest change alters the character of the composition."

(To George Thomson, publisher, Edinburgh.)

.   .   .   .   .   .

" Pure Church music ought to be performed entirely *by the voices only,* except for the *Gloria* or words of that kind.   That is why I prefer Palestrina; but it would be absurd to imitate him without possessing his spirit and his religious convictions."

(To the organist Freudenberg.)

• • • • •

" When your piano pupil has the proper fingering, the exact rhythm and plays the notes correctly, pay attention only to the style; do not stop for little faults or make remarks on them until the end of the piece. This method produces *musicians,* which after all is one of the chief aims of musical art. . . . . For the passage work (virtuosity) make him use all the fingers freely. . . . . Doubtless by employing fewer fingers a ' pearly ' effect is obtained—as it is put—' like a pearl.' But one likes other jewels at times."

(To Czerny.)

(The Baron de Trémont wrote in 1809, " Beethoven's piano playing was not very correct and his manner of fingering was often faulty ; the quality of his tone was not beyond reproach. But who could dream of the player? One was completely absorbed by the thoughts which his hands tried to express as well as they could.")

• • • • • •

" Amongst the old masters, only Handel and Sebastian Bach had true genius."

(To the Archduke Rudolph, 1819.)

• • • • • •

" My heart beats in entire concord with the lofty and grand art of Sebastian Bach, that patriarch of harmony (*dieses Urvaters der Harmonie.*")

(To Hofmeister, ʹ1801.)

• • • • • •

" I have always been one of the greatest admirers of Mozart, and I shall remain so until my latest breath."

(To the Abbé Stadler, 1826.)

• • • • • • ,

" I admire your works above all other pieces for the theatre. I am in ecstasy each time I hear a new work by you, and I take more interest in them than in my own. In brief, I admire you and I love you. . . . . *You will always remain the one I esteem most amongst all my contemporaries. If you wish to give me an extreme pleasure do write me a few lines. That would give me great satisfaction. Art unites everybody,* how much more true artists, *and perhaps you will consider me also worthy* of being counted one of this number."

(To Cherubini, 1823.)

(The words in italics are in French in the original with some
     defective spelling.   This letter to Cherubini was not
     answered.)

ON CRITICISM.

" In all that concerns me as an artist, no one has ever heard me say that I pay the least attention to what has been written about me."

(To Schott, 1825.)

.   .   .   .   .   .

" I think with Voltaire that mere fly-stings will not hold back a run-away horse."

(1826.)

.   .   .   .   .   .

" As for these idiots, one can only let them talk. Their prattling will certainly not make anyone immortal, any more than it will raise to immortality any of those whom Apollo has destined for it."

(1801.)

.   .   .   .

THE NINE SYMPHONIES

THE NINE SYMPHONIES

SYMPHONY No. 1 in C major, Opus 21.
Dedicated to the Baron van Swieten.

*Adagio molto—Allegro con brio—Andante canta-
bile con moto—Minuetto e Trio—Finale.*

Although this Symphony was originally performed at the first of the composer's personally-
arranged concerts in Vienna, on April 2nd, 1800,
the sketches for it extend over the preceding five
years. Though the symphony is in the composer's
first period style, it does not rank amongst the
very finest works of this period. The slow introduction starts on a dominant seventh out of the
key.

The musical quotations are taken from E. Pauer's excellent
piano solo arrangements of the Symphonies (Augener Ltd.).

The first movement proper is orthodox in form, and only once or twice do we catch a glimpse of the Beethoven to be, notably in the muttering bass passages near the end of the exposition. The *Andante* which is also in Sonata-form proper and opens fugally, contains some original drum-work. The Minuet, purely Haydnesque, shows a certain delight in orchestral colour.

In the trio the first chord is struck no less than nine times, as though the young composer was entirely occupied with the charm of his orchestral colouring. The *Finale* is not highly individual. The work is scored for strings, wood-wind, two horns, two trumpets and two drums.

2nd SYMPHONY in D, Opus 36.

Dedicated to Prince Carl Lichnovsky.

Adagio molto—Allegro con brio—Larghetto— Scherzo and Trio—Allegro molto.

In the Second Symphony, which is a great advance on the first, the composer's hold of his

subject is much firmer and the subjects themselves
are more striking.

The *Larghetto* is full of lovely curves,

and there is some charming conversational work
between the wood-wind instruments.   The horn
passage is the precursor of many fine symphony
subjects of a martial nature for the horns.

Whilst the chromatic harmony is purely Mozartian, the *Scherzo* is a genuine Beethovenian
outburst, full of verve and piquant in touch.

There is a feeling of broadness about the brilliant and energetic *Finale* which is absent from the
Finale of the First Symphony.

3rd SYMPHONY, Opus 35, " Eroica " in E flat.
Dedicated to Prince Lobkovitz.

Allegro con brio—Marcia funèbre—Scherzo and Trio—Finale.

This Symphony was completed in August, 1804, and first performed on April 7th, 1805. The French Ambassador at Vienna had suggested that Beethoven should write a work on the grand scale based on his admiration for Napoleon as the saviour of France from the horrors of the Revolution ; and it is a fact that Beethoven actually dedicated this Symphony to Napoleon, but when the news came that the First Consul had declared himself Emperor, Beethoven tore up the title page in a rage and added the following superscription : —

Sinfonia Eroica, composta per festeggiare il Souvenire di un grand' Uomo,
E dedicata A Sua Altezza Serenissima
Il Principe di Lobkovitz da Luigi van Beethoven,
Op. 55 No. III. delle Sinfonie.

This is one of the grandest and most powerful of the works in the Second Period style. It is noteworthy that all the principal themes are based on the intervals of the common chord, or on the little pendant of the diminished third which forms the tail of the first subject.

The work opens *in medias res* with two strong chords, the chief subject entering on the cellos.

There is some lovely responsive work between the wood-wind and the string bands for the second subject. The development is masterly and embraces a wonderful new subject, first entering on the oboes in the strange key of E minor. The recapitulation is approached in a marvellous way —the climax of the development being reached with a chord in C flat, the echoing reflections of which gradually die away until they reach a mere shimmering of violins, into which is suddenly thrown an unexpected entrance of the horn with the chief theme in the tonic key. Was it a slip? Of course not. Rather a stroke of genius. The movement has an immense *coda,* which with Beethoven at this period amounts to a second development.

The Funeral March is one of the grandest things in music. It is a pageant of a great world tribulation rather than an elegy for Napoleon, who was certainly not dead at that time. More probably Beethoven's mind was occupied with the

I

misery and wretchedness caused by war than with
the single hero of that period who reaped both glory
and dishonour at one blow. The oboe subject
in the Trio portion is only one of many wonderful
passages in this piece. The speaking bass melodies, the majestic second subject on the strings
almost bursting with eloquence, and the wonderful
coda, not broken-hearted but buoyed up by the
rhythm of things viewed broadly. Any attempt to
connect the *Scherzo* and *Finale* with Napoleon must
fail ludicrously. The *Scherzo* is simply one of
Beethoven's finest productions in one of his bubbling, vivacious mood. The three horns have a
subject which appears to be a genuine hunting call.

It is a seven-bar phrase, the echoes to which are
enchantingly coloured. The common chordal for-
mation of the duple time interjection near the end
suggests something more massive, and the little
coda figure, *E flat, E natural, F,* comes from the
opening theme of the Symphony. The *Finale* is
an amazing set of variations, the bass of the eight-
bar theme being displayed and varied many times
before the melody itself enters at the eightieth bar;
and even then we continually hark back to the

bass. It is not until the close, after the melody has been given at a slow rate on the wood-wind in its proper setting, that it is taken up triumphantly and carried victoriously into the coda. Beethoven used this particular theme four times—in a Contretanz, in his *Finale* to the *Men of Prometheus,* as the theme for his set of variations for piano, Opus 35 and in this Symphony. This curious method of writing a set of variations recurs 20 years later in the Ninth Symphony. A somewhat similar process has been adopted by Elgar in his *Enigma Variations,* as the theme used there is said to be the counter-subject of a concealed melody.

4th SYMPHONY in B flat, Opus 60.
Dedicated to Count Oppensdorf,

*Adagio—Allegro   vivace—Adagio—Menuetto—
Finale.*

This happy and serene work has been undeservedly overshadowed by its two towering neighbours. Schumann has called it a slender Greek maiden between two Norse giants. The opening *Adagio* sounds the only dark mood in the Symphony

It is lashed on to the *Allegro* by some powerful violin scales.

The flute, oboe and bassoon converse sportively over the second subject. A strange sequential passage in unison upon the strings in three-bar phrases following a happy little canon on the wood-wind instruments and some powerful syncopations lead in to the development. An atmosphere of humour and good feeling permeates the movement

The lovely melody which forms the chief theme of the *Adagio* is given to the violins. It is accompanied by a strong persistent rhythmic figure, which is transferred later on to the drums with great effect. The wood-wind work and the horn passages are exquisite.

The third movement *Allegro vivace* is full of fun, lively syncopations and duple time effects giving it more of the nature of a *Scherzo*.

It has a charmingly tender trio and a coda of
exquisite poetry ending with Schumann's "Just
one more question for the horn to put " before the
final crash.   This is one of the longest movements
which Beethoven has written in this form.   The
bright, sunny mood of the opening movements
increases in the radiant *Finale*.   There the modulations are surprising and the touches of humour
delightful.   The little skirmish on the part of the
bassoon just before the return, the whimsical little
notes on the flutes and violins, the augmentation
of the subject as it fades away into the stealthy
questionings between the violins and bassoons
near the end, are but a few of the many little
quips and sallies.

5th SYMPHONY in C minor, Opus 67.
Dedicated to the Prince von Lobkovitz and the
Count von Rasumovsky.

*Allegro con brio—Andante con moto—Scherzo
and Trio—Finale Allegro.*

This famous Symphony with its rugged first
movement, its lovely *Andante*, its mysterious
Scherzo and its proud, fiery *Finale*, was first performed together with the so-called Sixth Symphony on December 22nd, 1808. The Pastoral
Symphony No. 6 was probably written before the
5th.

The first movement opens without introduction with the famous phrase of four unison notes which Beethoven once explained as " Thus fate knocks at the door."

From this tiny germ the whole of this fierce stormy movement is evolved. Not even the beautiful tender second subject, nor the lovely little unbarred oboe cadenza can win it away from this rugged fierce mood. When this second subject appears in the recapitulation, still in the minor, the atoning major outburst which immediately follows is quickly brushed aside by the impatience of the reinstated first theme. Even the limitations of the old-fashioned horns and trumpets in those days seemed to be turned to advantage in the colossal bare thirds and fourths of the " Fate " notes.

The chief theme of the *Andante,* wonderfully sad, yet wonderfully beautiful,

is further enhanced by one of those majestic marching subjects which only Beethoven could conceive. The beauty of the wood-wind work is remarkable and the coda is full of strange fancies.

The *Scherzo* has some eloquent bass passages,

and its rhythmic horn figures are full of veiled mystery and heavy with some dark foreboding. The trio is a fiery *Fugato* with strange outbursts on the basses. The curious hesitations on its reappearance and the weird bridge passages at the end, with the long sustained chord on the strings and the mysterious drum tapping, cause the movement to veer gradually round to the fiery marchlike coda, with its light, graceful, contrasted episodes. The *Scherzo* theme insinuates itself into the *Finale* near the coda, which is of amazing brilliancy, ending with a *Presto* which fairly sweeps the hearer away with it.

The orchestra is the largest the composer has used so far. It includes three trombones, double bassoon, and piccolo, which, however, are only used for the brilliant *Finale*.

6th SYMPHONY (Pastoral) in F, Opus 68.

Dedicated to Prince von Lobkovitz and Count von Rasumovsky.

Pastoral Symphony, or a recollection of country life. More an expression of feeling than a painting.

Allegro ma non troppo—Andante molto moto— Allegro—Allegretto.

This Symphony, often slighted on account of its so-called realisms and its classification amongst "programme music," is, nevertheless, one of the finest pieces in the whole range of absolute music. The labelling of the various movements by Beethoven—"Joyous sensations roused by arrival in the country," "Scene by the brook," "Merry gathering of country peasants," "Thunderstorm," "Glad and grateful feeling after the storm"—is quite superfluous. How artistically Beethoven has introduced the bird calls—the quail, the nightingale, and the cuckoo—into just the right place —the coda of the *Andante*. And the thunderstorm. What a magnificent introduction to the *Finale* it makes! Beethoven has never once transgressed the great principles of form and balance in this Symphony.

The opening movement is a true country picture,

full of the tonics and dominants of summer happiness.

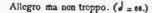

Bird-like twitterings and horn calls come from
all directions, yet how perfectly balanced it all is
and what a marvel of development! The scene by
the brook with its drowsy re-iterated figure on the
under-current of divided strings is the very Bourdon
ever sounding in Nature herself.

Wagner has not forgotten this in his *Woodland
Murmurs*. The dance of the villagers, founded
on the old country dances, is full of humorous
touches, the drowsy bassoon notes, the romp
round, and into this almost without warning,
breaks the storm. A remarkably controlled storm

it is, too, free from any vulgarity. A lovely bit of blue sky showing at the end, leads straight into the shepherd's song of thankfulness, which although containing several interesting points, the triple pedal at the opening with its horn yodel, etc., is somewhat lengthy and not very interesting. Beethoven had once intended to introduce words and chorus here, " Lord, we thank Thee," and it seems a pity that this idea was not carried out.

7th SYMPHONY in A major, Opus 92.

Dedicated to Count Moritz von Fries.

Poco sostenuto—Vivace—Allegretto—Scherzo— Finale.

This Symphony was completed in May, 1812, but was not performed until December, 1813, at a Concert undertaken by Maelzel for the benefit of the wounded soldiers at the Battle of Hanau, October 30th, which Concert also contained Beethoven's *Battle Symphony*. In form, the Symphony contains nothing unusual. In subject, it is full of romance and colour from beginning to end.

⌐ Opening with a long introduction, which is almost a movement in itself, this contains a strong marching figure, and runs into the *Vivace* by the means of a half cadence. The *Vivace*, a rhythmical

movement in 6-8 time, is full of a verve and
vitality which seems to reach its fullest power on
the horns and wind instruments with their tuckett-
ing rhythms.

Vivace.

The *Coda* amounts to a second development, and
the whole movement goes with a splendid swing
from beginning to end.

Rhythm but of another kind is also paramount
in the elegiac pageant-like movement designated
Allegretto, but curiously enough marked by
Beethoven himself at 76, by Maelzel's newly-
invented metronome.   It is a highly coloured
pageant, seen through a veil of mist, typified by
the wonderful six-four chord on the wood-wind
with which it commences and concludes.   The
structure of the *Scherzo* (here marked *Presto*) has
a strong relationship with its splendid fire and
strong duple time effects to that in the 6th
Symphony.   The romance of the Trio with its
wonderful low horn work is equally fine, and the
movement is broadened out to considerable length
by the return of the *Trio* and of the *Presto*, thus

making it a kind of Rondo—A, B, A, B, A—to say nothing of the humorous juxta-position of the two subjects near the end.

The *Finale* is also planned on the big scale, colossal in force and mighty in stride. There is a curious perversity of scale in the First Subject as though Beethoven was no longer satisfied with the ordinary major. The marvellous stride of the Bass at the end is not the least amazing of the features in this wonderful movement. Perhaps, this symphony holds together as one complete whole more than any other. It gives one the impression of having been written uninterruptedly from the first movement to last.

8th SYMPHONY, in F major, Opus 93.

*Allegro vivace e con brio—Allegretto—Presto—
Allegro vivace.*

"The little one," as Beethoven affectionately called this symphony, was written during four

months of the summer and early autumn of 1812.
It is smaller in scale, slighter in texture, than the
other symphonies. Erroneously regarded as a
return to an earlier style, and labouring for some
time under the absurd title of " Ballet-Symphony,"
it has been somewhat neglected in the past. Without the grandeur of the Fifth or the romance of
the Seventh, it contains a lasting, if less easy,
charm, perfect finish, and a rich fur.l of good
humour. Only a small orchestra is used, but it
is handled in a masterly way, as the octave drums
in the masterly finale, the charming *staccato* chords
for wood-wind with boisterous interjections from
the full orchestra, the running conversations between the violins and the basses, fully testify.

The first movement is in the usual development
form.

A sprightly *Allegretto* takes the place of the
slow movement. The third movement goes back
to the early minuet, instead of the Scherzo.

The final movement is a masterpiece of construction and development which its astounding interruptions so amply justifies finally.

Allegro vivace.

9th SYMPHONY, in D minor,
With Final Chorus on Schiller's " Ode to Joy."
(Op. 125).

Allegro ma non troppo un poco maestoso—Molto vivace—Adagio molto e cantabile—Choral Finale.

It is important to remember, as M. Romain Rolland has reminded us, that this is not a Choral Symphony in the strict sense of the term, but a " Symphony with a Final Chorus." The choral *Finale* was written by Beethoven in a separate MS., and, as with most of his other final movements, he seems to have expected no closer connection with the preceding three movements than that of general suitability. His original idea for a last movement to this Symphony was the Finale of the String Quartet in A minor, Opus 132, but for some reason or other his sketches for voices on Schiller's Ode were taken up again and worked into a *Finale* for this Symphony. Ten years had elapsed between the completion of the Eighth Symphony and the consummation of the Ninth, the colossal first three movements of which are on the highest plane of all music. As to the complete success of the choral numbers, opinions differ widely. The first movement, colossal in conception and dignified in tone, has moods of great passion and wonderful tenderness. The opening theme is mighty in aspiration, rugged in power.

The second movement is the *Scherzo,* one of Beethoven's longest, and perhaps his very finest. It is all brought about by the little germ theme of three notes, which, amongst other things, sug-

gests an unusual tuning of the drums in octaves.
A *fugato* follows, after which the second subject
enters in the unorthodox key of C major. It is
here that many conductors take upon themselves
to thicken Beethoven's wood-wind melody, with
the brass instruments. The *Trio* is built up on
a delightful double theme ushered in by the very
first entry of the bass trombone.

The *Adagio* opens with a melody of the utmost
nobility, perfect in curve, and of a marvellous
serenity.

A sudden modulation brings us to a new subject
in D major in 3—4 time.

The first subject then re-appears in G major, this is followed by a mystic passage in E flat major, in which fragments of the first theme appear after the manner of a dreamy meditation in which there is some magnificent work for the horn. The first subject then appears in the original key and gradually passes over into a solemn and majestic *coda*. The form is original, even with Beethoven.

Immediately a huge hubbub breaks out from the whole of the wood-wind instruments. A short hasty review of a few bars from each of the first three movements follows, and after the bass instruments had commented rather brusquely on these appearances, the famous tune in D major

breaks in on the cellos and basses alone. The melody gradually unfolds itself but finally is suddenly broken off by the discordant hubbub again, and the solo baritone voice enters with the words, " O brothers, not these tones."

The opening quartet and chorus is based entirely on the famous tune. The following number is a tenor solo and chorus to the accompaniment of a military band with all the appurtenances thereof—big drum, triangle and cymbals. A broad chorus follows, *Andante maestoso, a capella* in style; and as movement after movement enters, the

K

devout feeling of mysticism and awe increases, until the final chorus

Chant one greeting, myriads countless

caps with warm dazzling sunlight one of the highest peaks in all music.

THE PIANOFORTE SONATAS

THE PIANOFORTE SONATAS

1st SONATA, Op. 2, No. 1, in F minor.

The first Sonata has the usual four movements of the Haydn form : *Allegro—Adagio—Menuetto and Trio—Prestissimo*. The first and the last are in the usual Sonata form proper. The slow movement follows Mozartian lines. This Sonata is the first of the set of three in this Opus, which are all dedicated to Joseph Haydn, and the fact of such a superscription points to the respect which Beethoven had for the older composer, although he could not find it in his heart to continue with him long as his pupil. The whole of the Sonata, which appeared for the first time in 1796 and was probably written much earlier, is decidedly conventional in form, and shews us Beethoven starting on the lines laid down by those who went before him—Philip Emanuel Bach, Haydn, and Mozart.

The first movement is pure Haydn music, and the only glimmer of the future Beethoven comes in with that lovely little tune at the *Coda*. The development portion is thin and characterless. The first subject of the second movement was adapted from an early pianoforte quartet. A similar process was resorted to in the first movement of the third Sonata of this set for the second subject. The expression of this movement is not deep, nor does it sound that note of serenity which we regard as the chief characteristic of a Beethoven slow movement of the mature period.

The *Minuet and Trio* is purely Mozartian, especially in its double counterpoint and its inversion of parts. Some characteristic touches are found in the second subject of the last movement, which is in two parts, and the use of an altogether new subject in the development portion. This device is next used in the Sonata in F, Opus 10, No. 2—a device carried to great perfection in the development portion of the first movement of the *Eroica Symphony*. The use of this broad subject does away with any idea of development, although the movement is built up on a figure of three chords, a point referred to in both codas. The first part of the second subject has that weird, foreboding feeling, which we feel frequently in Schumann's music. Already he shews a striking fondness for the diminished third; but the passage is not particularly striking. Far otherwise is the beautiful little tune of eight bars which forms the second part of this subject.

2nd SONATA, Op. 2, No. 2, in A.

*Allegro vivace—Largo appassionata—Scherzo
and Trio—Rondo grazioso.*

There is a distinct advance in the second Sonata.
Although there are still the accepted four movements, the Minuet has now become a Scherzo.
This Sonata was probably written shortly after the
first, and in it we see how quickly Beethoven took
a firm hold of form and design in construction.
There is a feeling of considerable power about the
first subject, and its short, pithy figures promise
well for the development portion, a fact of which
Beethoven takes immediate advantage.

The second subject has a dual tonality, beginning in E minor and ending in E major. This,
of course, reappears in the final section in A minor
and major. There is considerable double counterpoint, and we have the characteristic rumblings in
the bass. The canon in three parts at the octave,
in the development portion, taxes the right hand
of most players. The recapitulation is shortened
and considerably altered.

In the *Largo Appassionata* we get very near to
the grandeur of Beethoven's middle style. The
opening subject has serenity, and there is scarcely
anything passionate in the whole movement which
breathes of solemn yet tender earnestness. This
movement may be regarded as either in Rondo
form or in Ternary form. There is a powerful

episode in flats near the end, but the music closes with an epilogue full of tender feeling.

We find a right boisterous joy in the *Scherzo,* which is evolved from one single little figure. The sequence of dominant seventh chords in the bridge, however, was already somewhat hackneyed even at that time.

The final Rondo is a graceful movement which owes much to Mozart. An episode leads to the second subject in E major, and this in its turn to the re-appearance of the first subject in varied form. Then comes a stormy episode in the minor which gradually subsides into the return of the first subject, then of the second subject, and finally winds up with a long *coda* containing reminiscences of all the subjects.

3rd SONATA, Opus 2, No. 3, in C major.

Allegro con brio—Adagio—Scherzo—Allegro assai.

This, the third of the set of the three early Sonatas dedicated to Haydn, appeared for the first time on March 9th, 1796, when Beethoven was twenty-six years of age. Eugen d'Albert regards this Sonata as essentially a virtuoso piece. This is saying rather much, although he is right in warning the interpreter against any attempts to render it mysterious by hyper-critical subtleties.

The first subject of the opening movement is a

typical Beethoven one, evolved from a short figure of two bars. Some brilliant passage work then occurs. It was certainly Beethoven's custom at this early period to regard such passages in a more physical sense. The second subject enters with a dominant minor section, followed by a major section, in which appears some fine canonic work. The minor part of this subject, which was adapted from an early pianoforte quartet which Beethoven had written in his youthful period, abounds in the turns and trills characteristic of that time. The broken octaves in the coda are frequently rendered now-a-days by alternate double octaves between the two hands in demisemiquavers.

The development is much more Beethovenish, containing some striking double octave cataclysms. There is also a very fine enharmonic change from an F minor chord to F sharp minor. The Coda is noteworthy as it includes some fine arpeggio effects and a striking slow *cadenza*.

The second movement, *Adagio* in E major, opens with one of Beethoven's dignified slow themes, which is sandwiched in Rondo fashion with disturbing episodes throughout. The first episode (in E minor) contains conversational work between the bass and the treble, the left hand crossing the right for the latter. At the end of the return of the first theme, there is a very striking example of an interrupted cadence—the dominant chord of E major being followed by the tonic chord of C.

The *Scherzo* (three-four time) is in C major, and should be taken at a fast rate. It is one of those movements which would have been better written in six-four time by running two bars into one.

The final movement is a grandiose Rondo—six-eight time—in C major, which requires a good technique, especially for the left hand. The second subject is somewhat conventional, but the next episode contains one of those lovely hymn-like tunes in which Beethoven delights. For the third episode, the subject of the first episode is repeated, but here in the tonic key; thus making the form what is known as Modern Rondo or Sonata Rondo, in contrast to the old Rondo in which every episode was different. The *Coda* is remarkable and is certainly of the virtuoso order. I never play it without thinking of the *Coda* to Mendelssohn's *Wedding March*. The sequences at the 15th bar after the *Vivacissimo* are not easy to finger. D'Albert fingers the upper part, 3, 4, 5, and the lower three notes with the thumb. Larger hands will produce a better effect by fingering the right hand top notes, 4, 5, 5, and the alto, 2, 1, 1. The triple shake near the end is frequently played by an alternation of six-four chords in either hand. There is a remarkable example of an interrupted cadence here, where D becomes D sharp leading to an A major chord. These unexpected rallentandos and calando before the strepitous rush home become a standing characteristic in Beethoven's music.

4th SONATA, Opus 7, in E flat.

*Allegro molto e con brio—Largo con gran espres-
sione—Allegretto Minore—Rondo.*

This Sonata which appeared for the first time
on October 7, 1797, is dedicated to the Countess
Babette von Keglevics. The composer, at the age
of twenty-seven was rapidly winning his spurs,
but still wrote on the old lines and with the cus-
tomary four movements. His Minuet however
has now become a lively movement and lost all
traces of its origin in the stately dance. It is quite
likely, however, that the Minuets of Haydn and
Mozart were also taken at a lively rate, incom-
patible with the dance.

The first movement in regular " Sonata Form "
is in six-eight time, in happy mood. The joyous
rhythm is occasionally emphasised by sforzando
syncopations. The subjects are all very taking,
and there are some striking modulations in the
development.

The *Largo* is full of religious calm. There is
a striking interrupted cadence at bar 19, and one
of those majestic march-like movements for the
second subject, which on its return at the end,
appears as a tenor melody. The movement is full
of rich colouring. The tones of the flutes and
other wood-wind instruments, may be imitated
in parts also the song of birds.

The first part of the *Allegro,* which takes the

place of the Minuet movement, is much more
extended than usual.   In place of the Trio, we
have a movement in the tonic minor of low broken
chords, full of that brooding sadness to which
Schumann and Brahms in later days became so
prone.   This is linked up, however, to the return
of the first joyous theme to which it forms an
effective foil.   The final Rondo in E flat is real
Mozart, and Mozart at his best.   Play the first
subject through, sixteen bars in length. Still the
bridge passage which follows is real Beethoven
He seems fairly obsessed with his little figure,
unable to let it alone, repeating it no less than
thirteen times in succession.   There is a virile
second subject.   The middle episode is stormy and
difficult to play unless one divines intuitively the
right action.   There is a remarkable enharmonic
change on the last page but one, where the tonality
is moved up a semitone from B flat to B natural
(a device of which the composer is fond), returning seven bars later on by the chameleon-like
" diminished seventh " chord.   Reference is made
in the *Coda* to the rhythm of the stormy middle
episode which is here turned to good use in the
brilliant peroration.

5th SONATA, Opus 10, No. 1, in C minor.

Allegro molto e con brio—Adagio molto—Prestissimo.

This Sonata is dedicated to the Countess von Brovne, and appeared for the first time on September 26, 1798. It is in three movements—the slow movement in A flat major.   There is no *Minuet* or *Scherzo,* the *Finale* instead being instilled with the spirit of the *Scherzo.*

The first movement is the usual development form, the first subject being composed in Beethoven's usual manner of two figures here, (a) upward flight, (b) soft chords.   It ends with a decided perfect cadence, the bridge subject entering after a bar's silence.   It is noteworthy that the second subject on its return appears in F major, before settling down finally into C minor.   This first movement, although in the minor, breathes a happy contented spirit, which deepens into seriousness in the Adagio.   This opens with a beautiful 16 bar phrase.   We then pass straight into the second subject, a florid one in a lighter vein of thought, closing in E major.   A sprinkled dominant seventh takes the place of the development section, and the whole is then repeated.   For the Coda, the first subject has passed into that serene happy atmosphere which only Beethoven's spirit seems to have penetrated.   The Finale is again cast into development form, and is typical of the way Beethoven expands his movements from the smallest idea. There is a beautiful hymn-like second subject. Characteristically enough, just before finishing this bubbling movement joyfully, the composer falls into a deep reverie, but only to brush it aside almost impatiently by returning to the original idea.

6th SONATA, Opus 10, No. 2, in F major.
Allegro—Allegretto—Presto.

The tenth Opus, which first appeared on September 26th, 1798, contains three Sonatas, all dedicated to the Countess von Brovne. The Sonata is in three movements—the first a movement of development, the second a *Scherzo,* and the third a playful *Presto.* The whole Sonata is cast in happy mood. The mysterious and somewhat eerie feeling of the Minuet being completely dispelled by the happiness of the Trio (which, curiously, enough, Brahms seems to have written over again in his Scherzo in E flat minor). The mood at the first part of this *Scherzo* has a close relationship with the *Scherzo* in the *Eroica Symphony.*

There are several noteworthy points about the development of the first movement. It opens with a treatment of the last three notes of the exposition in capricious manner. The development closes, too, with this idea, but it also contains a completely new subject in D minor. The prevalence of this tonality brings in the return section irregularly in D major. *The Presto* is one of those playful movements, full of fun and written broadly in Sonata form lines.

7th SONATA, Opus 10, No. 3, in D major.

Presto—Largo e mesto—Menuetto—Trio—Rondo.

This Sonata is one of the greatest works of the first period, if not, indeed, the greatest of them all. The first movement is a wonderful evolution from the first four-note figure, the development full of all kinds of strong devices, the stormy episode in the middle based on the rhythm of the opening phrase of the Sonata and the marvellous slow movement full of passion and tenderness, from its opening five-bar phrase to its beautiful close with those amazing tonic pedal chords. The spirited Minuet, really a *Scherzo* with two bars taken as one, is admirably contrasted with the Hunting Song of the *Trio*. Did Beethoven ever use the horse which Count Brovne gave him? The fine Rondo is cast on the old lines but filled with such new feeling.

The structure of the slow movement is in song form with five sections :—

(a) Theme in D minor in two parts with cadences in C major and A minor.
(b) Modulatory section from F to D minor.
(c) Theme in D minor with cadences in B flat and in D.
(d) Development of the (a) and (b) sections.
(e) Concluding portion.

8th SONATA, (Pathètique), Opus 13, in C minor.

*Grave—Allegro di molto e con brio—Adagio
cantabile—Rondo.*

Published for the first time in 1799, and dedicated
to the Prince Carl von Lichnovsky. Although
one of the few authentic titles, it is difficult to see
the meaning of its bearing of the Sonata as a whole,
unless indeed it is applied to the sad and dramatic
introduction theme which, indeed, deserves as a
leading motive to the first movement being introduced before the development section, and it ends
just before the coda. The slow movement is of
wonderful serenity and breathes a great religious
calm. Still, it was a great offence against good
feeling to make a double Psalm chant out of
it as one of our cathedral organists has done.
The Rondo does not quite reach the high plains
of the first two movements, it was probably
written much earlier; note the reflective mood again
just before the final whirlwind. There is no
Scherzo or Minuet in this Sonata.

9th SONATA, Opus 14, No. 1, in E major.

Allegro—Allegretto—Rondo.

The two Sonatas in this Opus, which is dedicated to the Baroness von Braun, are not very
interesting. No. 9 has no slow movement. The

meditative feeling having, apparently, crept into the *Allegretto,* which should again be taken as two bars in one. The Rondo in E is of great beauty and finish. The middle episode has again the feeling of a hunting song.

They appeared for the first time in December, 1799.

10th SONATA, Opus 14, No. 2, in G major.

Allegro—Andante—Scherzo. ˙

The first movement, in Sonata form, is a remarkable example of the growth of a whole movement from a single germ.

The Andante is an air with variations. The form of this is really ternary, although if the second part be repeated, it will throw the theme into five sections, A, B, A, B, A. The first variation places the air in the tenor, the second divides the harmony rhythmically, the third breaks up the harmony into semiquavers. Purists hold that this movement is wrongly barred throughout, the first beat coming where the third now is.

In the last sprightly movement, the *Scherzo* and *Finale* seem to have run into one.

The only other examples of Beethoven's use of the designation *Scherzo* for a movement not in Scherzo and Trio form are in the pianoforte sonata Opus 31 No. 3, and in the string quartet in C minor.

L.

11th SONATA, Opus 22, in B flat.

Allegro con brio—Adagio con molta espressione—
Minuetto—Rondo.

Dedicated to the Countess von Brovne.

This Sonata is the finest since the Opus 10, No.
3 in D. It is not so deep in feeling as some of
the preceding pieces, and the composer's pre-
occupation with development somewhat duly pro-
longs the first movement. It is full, however, of
characteristic vigour for its own sake, and the
Adagio, long-drawn as it is, possess a great charm.
This long-drawn meditative piece is the only case
in the Sonatas of a slow movement having all the
elements of the true Sonata forms—exposition and
development, recapitulation, coda. If the *Adagio*
breathes of the open country, the Minuet savours
of the salon. In this rather old-fashioned Minuet,
the *Trio* is styled "Minore." The Rondo with
four refrains, the last two varied.

12th SONATA, Op. 26, in A flat.

Andante con variazioni—Scherzo—Marcia funebre
—Rondo.

Dedicated to the Prince Carl von Lichnovsky.

This Sonata was announced for the first time on
March 3rd, 1802. Two of the movements are in
slow time—an Air with Variations, and a " Funeral

March on the death of a hero." The March is said
to have been written as a set-off to the popular one
of that day in Paer's opera, *Achilles*.

It is not a lamentation, but rather a tragic elegiac
picture set in an impressive frame. One feels the
throb of brass, the blare of trumpets, the roll of
muffled drums, the impressive pageantry of death.
The opening *Andante* is beautiful, and in the
variations the theme breathes as it were through a
thin lovely veil. The technique looks backwards
rather than forwards, and the movement ends
with a calm phrase. The final Rondo bubbles
with life ceaselessly until it disappears in a
faint whisper.

13th Sonata, Opus 27, No. 1, in E flat.

Sonata quasi una Fantasia.

*Andante—Allegro—Andante—Allegro molto e
vivace—Adagio con espressione—Allegro vivace.*

Dedicated to Princess Lichtenstein.

This Sonata was first published together with
the following one in C sharp minor on March 3rd,
1802. They were both composed in 1801, the happy
year of the composer's love for Countess Giuletta
Guicciadi. The term *Fantasia* by no means implies
formlessness, but rather a departure from the
ordinary Sonata form. The first movement—an

Andante, full of light and shade—is held by purists to be wrongly barred throughout, the first beat being the third, and so on. It is followed by an *Allegro* in C major which leads back to the return of the *Andante,* this time varied. The *Allegro,* which takes the place of the *Scherzo,* is full of imagination and vigour. The slow movement is used as a bridge leading into the *Finale.* All the movements are chained together in one whole. Just before the precipitant *Coda,* Beethoven takes a final glance back at the subject of the *Adagio,*

14th Sonata, Opus 27, No. 2, in C sharp minor.

Adagio sostenuto—Allegretto—Presto agitato.

The title page describes the work as *for clavecin or pianoforte.* The nickname, " Moonlight," given to it by the poet Rellstab, has no authority and only serves very faintly to define the peaceful charm of this sensitive picture, which was more probably inspired by the composer's romantic love for the Countess Giulietta Guicciardi. The direction in Italian, " to be played throughout with the greatest delicacy," is significant, although the term *senza sordini* is somewhat vague. It may have meant that it is to be played with the sustaining pedal, i.e., without the dampers. It is probably a general indication that the piece requires the pedal to sustain each harmony, for nowhere is harmony put to such effective use as in the dreamy yet placid opening *Adagio*. There is scarcely a stir, except where an occasional minor 9th causes a slight emotional ripple.

A little *Allegretto* takes the place of the usual Minuet. It might be a dance of peasants, heard in the distance. The restless and passionate *Presto* is one of the finest movements in all the master's works.

Like the preceding Sonata, all the movements follow on without break. But there is a definite organic connection between them, the *Finale*, and the opening movement in particular. Compare the first four semiquavers of the *Presto* with the second quaver group of the *Adagio*, and the quaver chords in the second bar of the *Presto* with the melodic figure in bars 5 and 6 of the opening movement.

The second subject of the *Finale* has three well-defined sections, the first melodic, the second dolorous expressive chords, the third a souvenir of the first. The *Coda* is one of the most deeply expressive things Beethoven has ever written. I' ends with a powerful gust of unpent passion.

15th Sonata, Opus 28, in D major.

Allegro—Andante—Scherzo—Rondo.

Dedicated to Joseph Eiden von Sonnenfels.

It was christened bv the Hamburg publisher, Cranz, with the name of " Pastoral Sonata." The autograph is dated 1801, and the work is exceeding happy in mood, the last two movements almost boisterously so, the *Finale* being a mad gallop home. This Sonata has four movements, and it is most probable that it was written before the two *Fantasia Sonatas*. The first movement opens with a phrase of nine bars over a gentle tapping tonic pedal. It is a splendid specimen of development by elimination and condensation. In the middle portion, just before the recapitulation, the phrase seems almost to disappear into thin air.

The *Andante* in D minor, with its epigrammatic *Trio* in the tonic major, was once a great favourite with the composer. The *Scherzo* which despite its title is really a *Minuet*, is one of his happiest, and the Rondo is full of the joy of field and forest.

16th Sonata, Opus 31, No. 1, in G major.

Allegro vivace—Adagio grazioso—Rondo.

This Opus contains three Sonatas—a favourite grouping with the composer. Although No. 1 was published in 1802, this Sonata, so simple in technique, has the feeling of having been conceived much earlier. The *Adagio*, with its elaborate flowery passages of no particular meaning, drops back to the Hummel style, and is developed to a considerable length. The Rondo is bright and sunshiny throughout.

17th SONATA, Opus 31, No. 2, in D minor.

Allegro—Adagio—Allegretto.

One of the most splendid of all Beethoven's Sonatas. The opening movement is full of the most speaking of all Beethoven's sonorous and passionate recitatives. The *Adagio* is in full binary form. It is very expressive, entirely evolved from a three-note figure, a little Hummelian. The final *Allegretto* is all spun out from the little four-note germ said to have been suggested to the composer by the cantering of a horse.

18th SONATA, Opus 31, No. 3, in E flat.

Allegro—Scherzo—Minuet and Trio—Presto con fuoco.

In this characteristic work, where we find both a Scherzo and a Minuet, the former in duple time, we again return to four movements. The mood throughout is of unclouded happiness. It is extremely interesting throughout, from the first bar which opens in an original manner with the " added sixth " chord to the Coda which returns to the same idea.

The *Scherzo* is in one of Beethoven's freakish moods, full of capricious turns and fun of all kinds. The third movement is a true Minuet of the olden style, whilst the *Presto* is one of those cantering movements the germ for which must have been derived from the hunting songs of the people.

19th SONATA, Opus 49, No. 1, in G minor and major.

Andante—Rondo.

This and the following Sonata, although published in 1802, must have been written much earlier; in fact, the theme of the G major Rondo was the original of the Minuet of the *Septet*.

20th SONATA, Opus 49. No. 2, in G major.

Allegro ma non troppo—Minuet and Trio.

This Sonata contains little of interest, both the Allegro and the Minuet are in the olden style.

21st SONATA, Opus 53, in C major.

Allegro con brio—Introduzione—Rondo.

This fine Sonata, too often made a mere piece of virtuosity, was dedicated to Beethoven's early friend and patron, Count Waldstein. The form is remarkable. A first movement, full of light and colour, and the romantic *Molto Adagio* forming an introduction to the final Rondo with its magnificent *Coda*. Beethoven originally intended the famous *Andante in F* for the slow movement of this Sonata, but finally discarded it in favour of the present slow introduction. The second hymn-like subject of the first movement does not appear in the tonic key, either in the exposition or in the recapitulation, but only after the final development near the end of the piece. The simple subject of the Rondo was the result as shown of six separate attempts in Beethoven's note-books. The whole meaning of it is lost unless the low C of the left hand is taken into the phrase. It will then be seen to have a close connection with the opening figure of the introduction. The full effect of the *Coda* is often lost by the preceding Rondo being taken too fast.

The *glissando* octave passage in it is very difficult on modern pianos on account of the deeper key fall.

22nd SONATA, Opus 54, in F major.

This remarkable Sonata, which appeared for the first time in April, 1806, is in two movements only —a *Tempo d'un Menuetto*, in full binary form (more like a Sonata movement than a Minuet), and a *Allegretto con moto* (somewhat Etude-like), with a *Prestissimo* Coda in which the hands very easily get tied up. This Sonata is comparatively little known, doubtless on account of its over topping neighbours, the *Waldstein* and the *Appassionata*. Bulow metronomed the opening movement at the quite moderate rate of 104 to the crotchet. The octave *bravura* subject appears there in its full majesty. The *cadenza* is noteworthy.

23rd SONATA, Opus 57, in F minor.

(Labelled *Appassionata* by the publisher Cranz).

Assai allegro—Andante con moto with variations —Allegro ma non troppo.

This Sonata, which was dedicated to Count Franz von Brunswick, is perhaps the most truly characteristic of all Beethoven's sonatas. The usual portrait of Beethoven with the massive jaws firmly set, the upturned eyes, the visage lined by suffering, the head of a Titan, might be quite appropriately placed here in the volume of the Sonatas, rather than at the beginning; for with the deep passionate note which sounds ceaselessly throughout the first movement and the immense vitality of the *Finale*, the calm beauty of the *Andante* with its variations, it holds the palm amongst all sonatas written for the clavier. Hackneyed it certainly is, but ever through the indifferent temperaments of mere finger players, the immense force of the ideas easily penetrates.

It is a superb example of the growth of Beethoven's immense creations from two of the tiniest of germs (a) the first three opening notes—C, A flat, F—(b) the C, D, C in the third and fourth bars. The whole sonata grows as naturally from these as the huge oak from the acorn. Bridge subjects, second subjects, coda figures, the chief theme of the *Andante*, as also the *impetuoso* subject of the *Finale*, are all derived from these two little germs. Lenz calls the Sonata "a volcanic eruption, which rends the earth and shuts out the sky with a shower of projectiles." The first movement and the last movement have truly immense *codas*.

For a clue to this sonata, Beethoven told an enquirer to read Shakespeare's *Tempest*.

24th SONATA, Opus 78, in F sharp major.

Adagio cantabile (4 bars)—Allegro ma non troppo—Allegro vivace.

This Sonata was composed in October, 1809 (considerably later than *L'Adieux Sonata*, which was published in July, 1811) and appeared for the first time in December, 1810. Thus an interval of five years separates it from the *Sonata Appassionata*. It was dedicated to the Countess von Brunswick, and the piece was a special favourite with the composer. A delightful feeling of happiness pervades the whole piece, and one cannot help feeling that this cheerful mood drew the composer to the choice of this radiant key. The first four bars form a sort of question to which the succeeding *Allegro* supplies the answer.

The movements are succinct in form, almost epigrammatic, and whilst very gracious and pleasing, are not hefty for all sorts and conditions of hands. The opening phrase of the Finale is very striking, so, too, is the coda with its wonderful disappointed cadence and its equally marvellous finish. The intricate work of the arpeggios relates it to the E major Sonata, Opus 109, and all the way through it, there is a curious oscillation betwixt major and minor modes.

25th SONATA, Opus 79, in G.

Presto alla tedesca—Andante—Vivace.

This is practically a Sonatina, and calls for little mention. Some authorities regard it as an unfinished sketch, whilst others ascribe it to a considerably earlier .date although it was clearly completed in 1809. The term *Tedesca* means " in the German style," and has reference to the country dance, *Ländler*. Beethoven employs the term only twice in his published works—here and in the fifth movement of the B flat quartet, Opus 130, where he describes the movement in one of the sketches as *Allemande Allegro*. In a Bagatelle, No. 3 of Opus 119, he uses the term in French, *A l'allemande*.

The first movement gives some good practice in crossing the hands. The second movement might easily be mistaken for a gondolier's song by Mendelssohn. The third movement is a lively *Con Moto* in simple Rondo form.

26th Sonata, Opus 81a, in E flat.

Adagio—Allegro—Andante espressivo—Vivacissimamente.

Styled by Beethoven himself, *Les adieux, l'absence, et la retour*. (The parting, the absence, and the return). As such it is the finest piece of programme music ever written. It is dedicated to his friend and patron, the Archduke Rudolph, but it is not known definitely that it was connected with the absence of the Archduke himself. The general feeling seems to suggest a more tender attachment. The music is Beethoven at his very best, and is truly representative of his mature period. The interrelation of the whole of the music, its close affinity with the opening musical motto of three notes, under which Beethoven wrote *Lebe-wohl* (Fare thee well) is astounding. Whether written in clear notes or obscured subtly, this leading motive lies at the bottom of every phrase. It is the generating idea, the essence of the whole Sonata. Although we have styled it programme music, it would be the greatest mistake, however, to regard it as something pictorial and definite. The idea is only used as the generating impulse of each of the three chief movements, and the work loses no whit (perhaps, even gains) by being heard as a piece of absolute music. Those interested in musical psychology will find it, however, a most interesting study to trace the derivation of the various phrases of the opening *Allegro* of the *Andante* (see bass chords), and even of the *Finale* to one of the two tiny cellules found in the first three bars of the introduction. The movements are all in Sonata form. The *Andante* has no development section and runs into the *Finale* without break.

27th Sonata, Opus 90, in E.

Con vivacità a sèmpre con sentimento ed espressione—Non troppo presto (Rondo).

This work, completed on August 16th, 1814, appeared for the first time in June, 1815. It is in two movements, and is one of the first works in which Beethoven gave bi-linguial *tempo* in-

dications (Italian and German), the other example
being *Les Adieux* Sonata, Opus 81. On one
occasion, in 1815, when the Englishman Neate
was discussing the meaning of music with Beethoven, the composer admitted somewhat vaguely
that he "never worked without a picture in his
mind." Be this as it may, the composer was
always greatly enraged when other people attempted to fix pictures to his music, as did the
publisher who gave the title "La chasse" to the
unchristened overture, Op. 115. The first movement has a tender wistful charm and romantic
feeling; it is the very poetry of sound. The first
subject with its three themes is square-cut, exactly
24 bars in length, ending with a perfect cadence
in the tonic key. The development is closely knit,
and the overlapping phrases with their diminuation
and augmentation, which bring in the return of
the first subject, are as wonderful as they are convincing.

Schindler relates that Beethoven, referring to
these two movements, said : "The first might
represent 'Combat between Heart and Head,'
and the second, 'Dialogue with the beloved one.'"
Be this as it may, the Rondo, judging from the
interior evidence, was written first. In many of
his sonatas the only connection apparently aimed
at between the various movements is that of right
contrast and suitable key-relationship.

28th Sonata, Opus 101, in A major.

*Allegretto ma non troppo—Vivace alla Marcia—
Adagio ma non troppo—Allegro risoluto.*

Dedicated to Freün Dorothea Ertmann and performed for the first time as new on February 18th, 1816; it was not published until February, 1817. With this Sonata we reach the third period of Beethoven's works, that in which reflection and philosophy play such a great part. Many passages in some of his latest works reach such a massive spaciousness that they seem to lose all touch of human comprehension. Beethoven was seeking a new style, in striving after which his music became more and more contrapuntal. One cannot help connecting his use of the fugue in many of his later works with this new phase. But it was not the fugue of Bach, but one filled with sublimity and mysticism in which he attempted to render the spiritual force more and more concentrated, the meaning sometimes becomes completely dissipated in his attempt to grasp and hold it. Such is not the case, however, with the fugue with which this Sonata ends. It grows out of the chief theme of the Finale and forms the development portion in this combination of the Fugue and Sonata form proper.

The martial feeling in the first movement seems to have produced a substitute for the *Minuet* or *Scherzo* movement. The *trio* with its prolonged

:oda is in deep poetic vein. The *Largo* is permeated with profound feeling and is connected with the *Finale* by a reminiscence of the first movement. The whole work is entirely happy and presents an untroubled frame of mind.

29th SONATA, Opus 106.

Allegro—Scherzo—A augio sostenuto—Fugue.

The first two movements were finished in April, 818; the two last were composed in the summer of 1at year. The Sonata was ready for publication 1 March, 1819, but did not appear until September, 1819. It carried the sub-title " Sonata for the Hammerclavier."[1] It is dedicated to the staunch friend and patron, the Archduke Rudolph, and is the longest of all Beethoven's sonatas, being about twice as long as the longest of the others. The first movement (over four hundred bars in length) is evolved from the two little germs contained in the first two bars. There is a long bridge passage in which derivative themes occur before the second subject in three sections. A long development follows and a superb return with a powerful coda. In the three bars preceding the return, all the " A sharps " are usually misprinted " natural." This A sharp should be the enharmonic of the following B flat.

The *Scherzo* is fantastic in the extreme. From

Beethoven could not endure the foreign word pianoforte.

M

the playful mood of the first part it is suddenly
plunged into the inexpressible anguish of the
minor trio. A short *Presto* unison phrase of eight
bars brushes this aside, a tremor on a minor ninth
preceding the happy return of the Scherzo.

The *Adagio* is one of the sublimest things in all
music. It certainly reaches heights which transcend
the limits of the piano. A remarkable passage,
which changes mood no less than six times, forms
a sort of prelude to the final fugue which is drawn
from the opening germ of the work. It is a
struggle of giants, unbridled in its onslaught.
Fuga a tre voci, con alcune licenze Beethoven
marked it, and its great licences and amazing con-
tortions have puzzled many minds. The heavenly
interludes, however, transport one into the pure
air of the *Sanctus* of the Mass in D. The simi-
larity of the opening phrases of the *Allegro*, the
Scherzo and the *Adagio*, should be noticed. It
was by such means that Brahms later on strove to
unify the separate movements of his longer forms.

30th SONATA, Opus 109, in E major.

*Vivace ma non troppo—Prestissimo—Andante
and Variations.*

Dedicated to Maximiliana Brentano.

Written at the age of fifty, it seems possible
that he poured into these later instrumental
movements much that he felt was beyond the

vocal forms of the great *Mass in D* which
was occupying his thoughts at this time. The
rhapsodic first movement with its light and happy
figures, repeatedly broken in upon by the deeply
expressive *Adagio* phrases; the remarkable uncouth Scherzo with the subject in the bass and the
angelic variations, one in fugue form, and the
other a *tour de force* with its thrilling pedals, the
beatific return of the theme at the end, given this
sonata a high place amongst the happiest concep-
tions of the master.

31st Sonata, Opus 110, in A flat.

*Moderato cantabile—Molto allegro—Arioso
dolente—Fuga.*

The autograph is dated December 25th, 1821,
and the work appeared for the first time in August,
1822. Here we find Beethoven in his most exalted
mood, and it is significant that whilst the main
outlines of the Sonata-form are at the foundation
of the piece, he has gone still a step farther in the
direction of welding the whole sonata into one
piece. The first, the movement of development,
is on the usual lines but is handled with great
freedom. The second movement is one of those
fast pieces, somewhat fantastic, with which
Schumann has made us familiar at a later period.
A remarkable *recitative* bridge portion follows
which leads into one of the most beautiful

airs ever penned by Beethoven, the *Arioso Dolente*. This runs into the Fugue, which is here used not so much as a movement in itself, but a concentration of the chief expression of the whole piece. Vincent d'Indy compares the expression here with that of the 15th String Quartet, Opus 132, written four years later, which contains the Song of gratitude to God for his goodness. In this Sonata, we have as it were a terrible combat against misfortune, then a return to life and hope, not in a calm pious prayer, but in an exultant hymn of joy triumphant.

The subject of the final Fugue is a simplification of the initial idea of the first movement. This opening movement is penetrated with a great religious calm. The *Scherzo* is somewhat puzzling, but appears to be a somewhat sorrowful frolic, a rather bitter amusement. In the Fugue, suffering disappears; even fantastic cleverness comes to the fore with the subject in contrary movement. Little by little life and joy return, and with the re-establishment of the tonic key, the piece triumphs in an enthusiasm of good feeling. The Italian indications to this sonata are fuller and more unusual, and show that Beethoven was aiming at the deepest possible expression. The use of the *Una Corda*, and the insertion of the *Arioso Dolente* into the Fugue, show what a struggle Beethoven underwent in the conquest of his feelings.

32nd SONATA, Opus 111, in C minor.

Maestoso—Allegro con brio—Arietta

Although the designation *Sonata* persists with
Beethoven right along throughout all his periods,
yet in this last sonata we have left the first
ones completely out of sight. The name must be
taken merely in its general sense of a piece of
high aims; or even in its literal sense, the Italian
word meaning simply *to play*. This Sonata, which
was dedicated to the Archduke Rudolph, is practically a Prelude and Fugue, with an Air and
Variations. The introduction contains two themes,
a leonine, stormy one and a singing phrase. The
Fugue opens like a veritable thunder-storm. There
are short phrases in the major which answer to the
second subject, a brief snatch of two celestial bars,
and the agitated atmosphere again unfolds itself.
This second subject, which is a mere phrase, is
repeated in the last portion of the Fugue in the
tonic major, which brings the Fugue into line with
the Sonata form proper. The beauty of the Coda
has not been surpassed by Brahms in his sublimest
moments.

After the storm, a calm. Beethoven concludes
his world contribution of Sonatas with an air of
celestial happiness, varied in the most lovely
manner possible. "A voice from above," someone
has called it. The variations lap round it tenderly
like the waves caressing the sands on a beautiful

calm day. The first variation gently stirs the rhythm of the theme. The second doubles the movement, and the third redoubles, and yet the peaceful calm is not disturbed. Into the *Coda* steals one of those beautiful pensive movements in the minor key. This emerges into the return of the theme, scintillating with heavenly radiance. Thus Beethoven closes his Sonatas in a heavenly peace.

THE SONATAS FOR VIOLIN AND PIANOFORTE

THE SONATAS FOR VIOLIN AND PIANOFORTE

1st SONATA, Opus 12, No. 1, in D.

Allegro con brio—Tema con Variazioni—Rondo.

This is the first of a set of three Sonatas published in 1799, and dedicated to F. A. Salieri. It is noteworthy that it was a favourite custom with Beethoven to publish his works in sets of threes; thus, Opus 1, Three Trios for Pianoforte, Violin and Cello; Opus 2, Three Sonatas for Pianoforte; Opus 9, Three Trios for Strings; Opus 10, Three Sonatas for Pianoforte; Opus 30, Three Sonatas for Pianoforte and Violin; Opus 31, Three Sonatas for Pianoforte; Opus 59, Three Quartets for Strings (dedicated to Prince Rasumovsky); and the Opus 12.

No. 1 of this Opus is a vivacious work of no great depth, and the phraseology is in the Mozartian manner. The theme is a 16-bar phrase, given out by the piano and repeated on the violin in two sections. The variations are four in number, the third being in the minor, and there is a short Coda. The Rondo is on modern lines approximating to Sonata form.

2nd SONATA, Opus 12, No. 2, in A.

*Allegro vivace—Andante più tosto Allegretto—
Allegro piacevole.*

Although this Sonata offers no outstanding
point of interest, it is to be regretted that it is
not more frequently heard. There are one or two
places where the sunny sky is slightly overcast,
but on the whole, it is a work brimful of youthful
happiness. The *Andante,* somewhat frail, is like
the *Finale,* full of fine melody, and gay with op-
timistic feelings of youth.

3rd SONATA, Opus 12, No. 3, in E flat.

*Allegro con spirito—Adagio con molto espressione
—Rondo.*

The tuneful, breezy *Allegro* contains some
brilliant work for the piano. The *Adagio* seems
hardly deep enough to carry its broad time with
dignity. The delicate Finale—short, simple, and
tuneful—is well rounded off.

4th SONATA, Opus 23, in A minor and major.

Presto—Andante—Scherzo—Allegro molto.

This Sonata, published in 1801, and dedicated
to the Count Moritz von Fries, is one of the more
serene works of the " first-period " style. Its
charms are not readily apparent, but it is full of
interest to the serious musician. The subjects of

the opening *Presto* are not very distinguished. The composer seems to have felt this, and has consequently introduced an unusual amount of new matter into the development section. The gentle, placid *Andante*, with its eloquent rests, has some unusual passages, notably the bridge (bar 33) where a definite theme is treated fugally in three parts. The Finale, undefined, strange and unusual, possesses that weird note which so frequently sounds in Schumann's pieces. The key of A minor seems to possess the right key-colour for this bustling, indefinite, and somewhat uneasy sort of mood. In this direction, one calls to mind the *Kreutzer Sonata*, with which this movement has much in common. There are more subtle reminiscences; the new theme in semibreves, which plays such a great part in the middle of the Rondo, recalls the fugal *Finale* of Mozart's *Jupiter Symphony*. The powerful *Coda* recalls all the foregoing moods. The movement is very valuable from the psychological point of view, for Beethoven was at the age of 31 years.

5th SONATA, Opus 24, in F.

*Allegro—Adagio molto espressivo—Scherzo—
Rondo.*

This graceful and happy Sonata, also published in 1801 and dedicated, like its predecessor, to the Count Moritz von Fries, is the most popular in the " early-period " style. The first movement is full of serene happiness. The Adagio has a lovely theme, dreamy and languorous as a summer's day. The *Scherzo* is characteristic, full of fun and oddity; the Rondo, full of good spirits, the chief theme being varied at each return.

6th SONATA, Opus 30, No. 1, in A.

Allegro—Adagio molto espressivo—Allegretto con variazioni.

This is the first of a set of three Sonatas dedicated to the Kaiser Alexander I. With this Opus the true individuality of Beethoven is manifested. Although the opening of this work is not particularly striking, yet the movement has a clarity of style and delicacy of workmanship together with distinct melodic charm. The theme of the *Adagio* is of great beauty, caressing in its tenderness. For the *Finale*, Beethoven turns to his beloved Variations form. This was not the original Finale which was " lifted " in a moment of haste to form the conclusion of the Kreutzer Sonata. Still, one cannot deny that the present variations suit this charming poetical sonata much better than the *Finale* of the *Kreutzer* would have done.

7th SONATA, Opus 30, No. 2, in C minor.

Allegro con brio—Adagio cantabile—Scherzo—Allegro.

This favourite work is one of the great masterpieces of music. The first and last movements sound the clear note of Beethoven's personality—a king here comes to his own. The first movement opens with a veritable quatrain of musical poetry. The gay martial swing of the second subject is remarkable. Stormy episodes follow, and the development section commences with a new idea. Conflict succeeds conflict before the serenity of the exposition returns. The beautiful *Adagio* flows along with a solemn majesty, although there are one or two short dramatic points. The *Scherzo*, bright and tuneful, somewhat naive, does not give us the fulness of the real Beethoven which we get in the sombre, energetic and passionate *Finale*.

8th SONATA, Opus 30, No. 3, in G.

Allego assai—Tempo di Minuetto—Allegro vivace.

After the stormy power and the serene beauties of the Sonata in C minor (a key which always called forth Beethoven's best) this Sonata appears somewhat colourless. The long-drawn *Tempo di Minuetto* is a little tedious, whilst the first and last movements, though vigorous and well varied in mood, by no means give us the deep Beethoven of the C minor Sonata. The scoring of many of the passages is unusually thin, and reminiscent of Haydn not at his best.

9th SONATA, Opus 47, in A.

Dedicated to Rudolph Kreutzer.

Adagio—Presto—Andante con variazioni– Presto.

Though absurdly over-estimated, perhaps on account of Tolstoy's stupid novel, this still remains one of the great masterpieces in music. Commissioned by a Mulatto violinist named Bridgetower, and written, as the original title-page says, " in a specially brilliant style," it was first given at 8 o'clock on a May morning in 1803 in the Augarten at Vienna, with Beethoven at the piano and Bridgetower with the violin. The Sonata opens with a majestic introduction, ending on a dominant pause. Tradition has it that Bridgetower improvised a cadenza here and that Beethoven approved. Amongst the whirl and excitement of the bold and vigorous opening *Presto*, the hymn-like second subject stands out with a marvellous way. Nothing is lost of the tenderness of the *Andante* in the brilliant variations which follow it, and this is all the more wonderful because this piece is the most virtuoso-like of all Beethoven's chamber-music. Tenderness with Beethoven is no maudlin sentiment, but the gentle sympathy of a strong man. The Tarantelle-like *Finale* originally belonged to the Sonata of Opus 30, No. 1, A major, but, as Beethoven had been dilatory in his commission, the time having arrived and no *Finale*, he took the *Finale* from the earlier Sonata and wrote a new one for it later on.

10th Sonata, Opus 96, in G.

Allegro moderato—Adagio espressivo—Scherzo allegro—Poco Allegretto.

This was written in 1810 and dedicated to Beethoven's firm friend and patron, the Archduke Rudolph. Although not really characteristic of the master's latest style, which does not commence until Opus 106, yet it is the most intimate of all the violin sonatas. It stands amongst the very great works and is indeed in some ways superior to the C minor. The *Adagio*, calm and sublime, is one of the most beautiful things in music. The scoring is like that of a string quartet. The ending dies away and creeps almost imperceptibly into the *Scherzo* through an unexpected C sharp. Full of life and bubbling over with fun, it has a

jolly *triu* and a *coda* of its own.   The *Finale*
touches every mood from gay to sad, from lively
to severe.   The lovely *Adagio* makes a re-appearance in it, but the gay mood wins, for with a
freakish little *Presto* the Sonata is brought to a
triumphant close.

THE STRING QUARTETS

THE STRING QUARTETS

1st QUARTET, Opus 18, No. 1, in F.

Dedicated to Prince Lobkovitz.

*Allegro con brio—Adagio affettuoso ed appassio-
nato—Scherzo—Allegro.*

Composed in 1800 at the age of 30, this first set
of quartets belongs to the same period as the great
C minor Symphony, No. 5. The music of No. 1
is Mozartian in type, very charming, and the
scoring is light and graceful. The *Adagio* is very
beautiful, and one can feel in it the future Beethoven. Indeed we almost arrive at maturity in the
episode in D flat in the *Finale*, where Beethoven
uses the melody which he again took up in his
ballet " The Men of Prometheus " and in his
Third Symphony.

2nd QUARTET, Opus 18, No. 2, in G. major.

*Allegro—Adagio cantabilo—Scherzo--Allegro
molto quasi Presto.*

This quartet is even more like Mozart and
Haydn than No. 1, except for the fact that Beeth-

179

oven keeps his music in rather higher registers. The *Adagio* is not so Beethovenish as the slow movement of No. 1, but it contains an episode marked Allegro. The *Finale* is full of spirit, but it is not the Beethoven in the "unbuttoned" mood of the later works. There is some effective work for the G string on the 1st Violin, for Paganini had already cast his glamour over Europe.

3rd QUARTET, Opus 18, No. 3, in D.

Allegro—Andante con moto—Allegro—Presto.

This beautiful quartet, composed a year later than the first two, already points to the maturity of the second period, especially in the first movement. The *Andante* opens with a lovely melody for the 2nd Violin on the G string; restraint and broadness in playing should be the player's aim here. Parry refers to the fine balance of form in this Quartet in his article in Groves' Dictionary. The *Scherzo* is here marked *Maggiore—Minore—Maggiore*. The *Presto* is full of Beethoven spirit and handling, in one passage in particular, having spaciousness, which is such a striking feature in the final quartets.

4th QUARTET, Opus 18, No. 4, in C minor.

*Allegro ma non tanto—Scherzo--Menuetto—
Rondo.*

Written in Beethoven's favourite key, C minor,
this quartet is remarkable for its melodiousness.
It has no slow movement and contains both a
Scherzo and a Minuet, the former marked Andante
Scherzoso quasi Allegretto and opening in a Fugato style reminiscent of the Andante of the First
Symphony. Both this and the Minuet contain
the characteristic Sforandi, especially that on the
third beat of triple time. The Prestissimo Coda
brings the Finale to a powerful conclusion.

5th QUARTET, Opus 18, No. 5, in A.

Allegro—Minuet—Air and Variations—Allegro.

This quartet is chiefly remarkable for its lovely
Andante and set of variations on the beautiful
theme which has all the natural feeling of a
genuine folk-song. The first variation is *Fugato;*
the second has sparkling triplets for the 1st violin; the third woodland murmurs, whilst the
cellos and violas occupy themselves with the
melody.

The fourth is organ-like in treatment, whilst the
final one starts on a boisterous scamper home,
which ends, however, in a melancholy, dreamy
meditation. The *Finale* is Mozartian.

6th QUARTET, Opus 18, No. 6, in B flat.

Allegro con brio—Adagio ma non troppo—
Scherzo—La Malinconia—Allegretto quasi
Allegro.

This favourite quartet, composed in 1800, has five movements; whereas the fourth quartet has no slow movement.

The arrangement of the five movements seems to suggest some sort of carefully-arranged " programme;" but woe always overtook the man who dared to attach a definite story to any of the music in these pieces in Beethoven's lifetime. The opening movement, full of vitality, and asks for *spiccato* bowing. It is very light in texture. The first *Adagio* is full of graceful tunefulness, somewhat elaborate in texture, and containing many characteristic touches of expression; so too, does the *Scherzo*. The second slow movement *Adagio,* entitled by Beethoven *La Malinconia* (grief), is one of Beethoven's most moving pieces of music. Knowing here that he was entering into new territory, he especially marks such movements to be played with the greatest feeling *piu gran delicatezza*. This movement runs directly into the final *Allegretto,* which indeed returns to it twice, as though unable to throw off completely the bitter taste of those sad moments.

7th QUARTET, Opus 59, No. 1, in F.

No. 1 of the set dedicated to Count Rasumovsky.

Allegro—Allegretto Vivace e sempre Scherzando—Adagio molto e mesto—Thème russe con Variazioni.

This fine but difficult quartet, sometimes called the Cello Quartet on account of the prominence given to this instrument, was written in 1806. The Count himself is supposed to have played the cello, and the set of variations on the Russian song used for the *Finale* was a second compliment to Beethoven's noble Russian patron.   Beethoven took his theme from the Prabst collection, 1815, which is not now published, having been superseded by Rimsky-Korsakoff's fine collection.   The theme is found there (No. 13) marked *Andante* and the Russian words may be translated—

> Ah, is this my fate?
> And what a fate!

The technique and the subject matter is very much more advanced.   The first movement contains a remarkable unison passage for the full strings, some remarkable high work for the 1st violin and some wonderful colour effects.   The *Allegretto* is a busy, gossipy movement in B flat.   The *Adagio molto* is a typical Beethoven *Adagio*.   It is the real thing.   It runs into the Finale through a long

and difficult cadenza for the 1st Violin over a
dominant pedal. The ending of the quartet contains some very full effects and is almost orchestral
in style.

8th QUARTET, Opus 59, No. 2, in E minor.

Allegro—Adagio—Allegretto—Finale.

The second quartet of the Rasumovsky set
is even more elaborate than the first. The opening movement, though containing some dark,
passionate moods akin to the *Appassionata Sonata,*
is nevertheless happy and delicate in tone.   Its
technical requirements are great.   The quartet
opens with two strong chords, then a silent bar,
which the composer fills in curiously enough in
the recapitulation. The lovely long-drawn Adagio
in E major is marked by Beethoven *con molto di
sentimento* (with great feeling).   Here again he is
in his new territory.   It is as though he said to the
players, " Wake up ! this is an entirely new kind
of music."   The playful *Allegretto* introduces
another Slav folk-song, which can be found in
Rimsky-Korsakoff's collection (No. 45).   It is
sacred and majestic in tone, a song of glory to
the Creator.   It forms the major *trio* portion,
which is carefully welded on to the return of the
opening minor movement.   The *Finale* represents
Beethoven's very happiest mood.   It starts clean

out of the key in C major. Seldom is Beethoven so happy as we find him here in the *Finale,* which although written in the sharp signature throughout, is really in the key of C major; the episodes only and the coda only just managing to restore the balance of E minor.

9th QUARTET, Opus 59, No. 3, in C major.

Introduzione—Allegro vivace—Andante con moto —Menuetto—Allegro molto (Fuge).

This, the third of the Rasumovsky set, was composed in 1806. Starting clean out of the key, a few bars of *Andante* introduction gradually lean towards C major. The first movement is remarkably clear and lucid in style and finely coloured in harmony. Beethoven is in one of his happiest moods. The exquisite *Andante* in A minor opens with a *pizzicato* bass and ends in the same manner. It is a highly finished movement. The Minuet is of the stately dance order and appears in the tonic key C major. The coda to it ends on the dominant seventh, thus bringing in the remarkable spiccato Fugue which Brahms played from memory as an encore at a concert in Vienna in 1867. The *Una Corda* set of entries preserving the homogenuity of tone and adding greatly to the effect of the intensity of the *crescendi* is particularly fine.

10th Quartet, Opus 74, in E flat.

*Poco adagio—Allegro—Adagio ma non troppo—
Presto—Allegretto con variazione.*

This remarkable quartet, composed in 1809 and
dedicated to the Prince Lobkovitz, is widely
known under the title of the Harp Quartet on account of the remarkable pizzacato arpeggios in
the opening Allegro. A short introduction is
marked *sotto voce*. The *Allegro* contains a brilliant cadenza for the Violin—Beethoven's only
excursion into the virtuoso field in chamber music.
The very beautiful *Adagio* is Beethoven at his
very best, whilst the *Presto Scherzo* is curious in
form, being arranged with varying *tempi*, thus,
on the following plan :—*Presto* C minor, *Più
Presto-Trio* C major, C minor, *Presto* repeated,
and again the C major, finishing with the C minor.
This leads without break into a set of six variations : the second, notable for its lovely viola
melody ; and the sixth, organ-like in character over
a cello pedal-point.

11th Quartet, Opus 95, in F minor.

*Allegro con brio—Allegretto ma non troppo—Al-
legro assai vivace ma serioso—Allegretto agitato.*

This quartet is dedicated to Count Zmeskal,
Beethoven's willing secretary and man of affairs.
Here in this work which stands on the border line

between Beethoven's second and third styles, we have the gruff and brooding Beethoven. The somewhat short opening movement is full of intense feeling. The *Allegretto* is calm and religious, ethereal in tone and contains a fine fugato passage. The third movement, which takes the place of a *Scherzo,* is dark in feeling and pervaded with gloom. A short *Larghetto* introduction leads into the *Finale* agitated and restless in character, but ending with a brilliant gleam of sunshine.

12th QUARTET, Opus 127, in E flat.

Dedicated to Count Nicolas von Galitzen.

Maestoso—Allegro—Adagio—Scherzando vivace—Finale.

Although probably published before his death, this quartet is generally classed with the posthumous ones which represent fully Beethoven's third style. Although all these quartets contain many orchestral effects, yet he never exceeds the limits of the true string quartet style. To say that string quartet writing is only an imperfectly filled-in sketch of orchestral idium is not correct; otherwise, when Beethoven had four instruments at his disposal, would he have written some of those spacious passages for three, or even two instruments only?

The opening movement has a double subject—

the *Maestoso* introduction accompanying the *Allegro* subject on every appearance. The *Adagio* is dreamy in mood and has a touching *Andante* episode, also a striking excursion to E major before the final return. The *Scherzando vivace,* which must not be taken too quickly, is also a striking example of Beethoven's characteristic contrapuntal writing and contains a passage in Beethoven's famous *Ritmo di tre battute* (Rhythm of three bars); another instance of this occurs in the *Ninth Symphony.* The tempo is constantly changing throughout and the highly dramatic music, free in style, settles down more into a lyric and rhythmic style for the *Finale,* the long *coda* of which is extremely characteristic, starting right away from the key.

13th QUARTET, Opus 130, in B flat.

Dedicated to Count Nicolas von Galitzen.

Adagio ma non troppo—Allegro—Presto—Andante con moto—Danza alla tedesca—Cavatina—Finale.

This quartet, written in 1825, is one of Beethoven's longest, and contains six movements. The opening piece carries its *Adagio* introduction through all the appearances of the *Allegro* subject. The second subject is of wonderful beauty. The development section very short. The unusual *Presto* in B flat minor very succinct; is the nearest approach to Brahms. The *Andante* is really a *Scherzo* treated like an *Andante* in form. The third movement is cast in the rhythm of a German country dance; the theme is varied on its reappearance. The famous *Cavatina* has a remarkable *beklemmt* (fear) episode and a wonderful *Bebung* chord at the close. The lovely second subject of The *Finale* has been used by Borodin as a theme in the *Finale* of his Second Quartet. There is a very proper little Fugue in the development portion. The original *Finale* was published separately as Opus 133; it is a terrificly long-drawn Fugue and is regarded as almost incomprehensible by even the most ardent admirers of Beethoven's third style.

14th QUARTET, Opus 131, in C sharp minor.

Published in 1827.

Adagio—Allegro molto vivace—Allegro moderato —Andante—Presto.

Although marked off in separate movements, this quartet is practically one long continuous piece. It opens with a mystic Fugue, organ-like in character and contains several fine enharmonic changes of key. At the *Allegro molto vivace* the tonality is lifted a semitone. This movement is light in character and simple in texture, almost Mozartian. An air with variations is approached by a *recitative* and introduction. This is followed by a *Presto*, where Beethoven appears in one of his joking moods. The *tempo* here alters continually, then comes a short *Adagio* section, a lamentation broken off by one of Beethoven's gruff shrugs, and the last movement opens with a clearly marked theme in happy mood. Strongly contrasted portions occur from time to time, but the work ends triumphantly.

15th QUARTET, Opus 132, in A minor.

Assai   sostenuto — Allegro — Allegro   ma   non tanto—Molto   adagio—Andante—Alla   marcia— Allegro appassionata.

The opening movement is on the same lines as that of the preceding quartet. Moods change constantly and the development is of the freest kind; there are two parts to the second subject, one a vivacious little figure, two a short singing phrase. The *Allegro* in A major is in terary form and takes the place of the *Scherzo.* Then follows that remarkable movement in the Lydian mode headed " A convalescent's sacred song of thanksgiving to the divinity." This interesting modal piece was written after the composer's illness. The variations of it alternate with the *Andante* in D major, thus producing striking contrasts of key colour. The final *Allegro* is in free Sonata form

16th QUARTET, Opus 135, in F major.

Allegretto—Vivace—Lento assai—Grave ma non troppo tratto.

This quartet is on a much smaller scale. The opening movement, whilst characteristic of the third period, is easily comprehended. The subject of the slow movement is one of Beethoven's most beautiful melodies, and the *Finale* commences with the famous musical motto—

> " *Must it be?*
> *It must be* "

founded on a little altercation with his cook.

The movement is characterised by some very perverse part-writing.

These final quartets present many problems, even to the most profound students of Beethoven's works.

BIBLIOGRAPHY

BIBLIOGRAPHY

If one wishes to know Beethoven better, reference should be made to the principal biographies and other works on Beethoven, of which we give a brief list :—

I.—FOR BEETHOVEN'S LETTERS.

LUDWIG NOHL.—*Briefe Beethovens,* 1865, Stuttgart.

LUDWIG NOHL.—*Neue Briefe Beethovens,* 1867, Stuttgart.

LUDWIG RITTER VON KOECHEL.—83 *Original Briefe L.V.B. an den Erzherzog Rudolph,* 1865, Vienna.

ALFRED SCHOENE.—*Briefe von Beethoven an Marie Graefin Erdody, geb. Graefin Niszky und Mag. Brauchte,* 1866, Leipzig.

THEODOR VON FRIMMEL.—*Neue Beethoveniana,* 1886.

Katalog der mit der Beethoven—Feier zu Bonn, an II.—15 Mai, 1890, verbundenen Ausstellung von Handschriften, Briefen, Bildnissen, Reliquien Ludwig van Beethovens. Bonn, 1890.

LA.MARA.—*Musikerbriefe aus funf Jahrhunderten.*
Leipzig, 1892.
DR. A. CHRISTIAN KALISCHER.—Neue Beethoven,
Briefe. Berlin and Leipzig, 1902.
DR. A. CHRISTIAN KALISCHER.—*Beethovens
Sämmtliche Briefe.* Kritische Ausgabe mit
Erlauterungen, 5 vol. Leipzig and Berlin,
1906-1908.
DR. FRITZ PRELINGER.—*Beethovens Sämmtliche
Briefe und Aufzeichnungen,* 3 vols. Vienna
and Leipzig, 1907.

By far the most useful books for the English
reader, and, indeed, for any reader, are the two
splendid volumes of *Beethoven's Letters.* A
critical edition with explanatory notes translated
from Kalischer by J. S. Shedlock. (London : J.
M. Dent & Co., 1909).

The translation of the letters contained in this
present volume have been taken from that work
by kind permission of the author and the
publishers.

A good selection from these letters, issued in
one volume at a moderate price, would be a great
boon to English readers.

II.—FOR BEETHOVEN'S LIFE.

GOTTFRIED FISCHER.—*Manuscrit* (especially interesting for the childhood of Beethoven). Fischer, who died in 1864, was the owner of the house where the Beethoven family lived for two generations. He and his sister Cecilia knew Beethoven as a boy intimately, and have recorded their remembrances of him, which are very valuable, on condition that they are used with some criticism. The manuscript is in the Beethovenhaus at Bonn. Deiters (see below) has published some extracts from them.

F. G. WEGELER and FERDINAND RIES.—*Biographie Notizen über Ludwig van Beethoven* (especially valuable for the first part of his life), Coblentz. 1838. Re-issued by Dr. Kalischer in 1905.

LUDWIG NOHL.—*Eine stille Liebe zu Beethoven.* Berlin, 1857. (A publication of the Journal of Mlle. Fanny Giannatasio del Rio, who knew and loved Beethoven about 1816).

ANTON SCHINDLER. — *Beethovens Biographie.* 1840. (For the second part of his life).

ANTON SCHINDLER.—*Beethoven in Paris, Münster,* 1842.

GERHARD VON BREUNING.—*Aus dem Schwarz-spanierhause*, 1874. (The Schwarzspanierhaus was the house in Vienna in which Beethoven died. It was pulled down during the winter of 1903).

MOSCHELES.—*The Life of Beethoven*, London, 2 vols. 1841.

ALEXANDER WHEELOCK THAYER, and continued by HERMANN DEITERS, and later by HUGO REIMANN.—*Ludwig von Beethovens Leben* (Translated into English), 5 vols., 1908. This biog 'phy was commenced in 1866, but was interrupted by the death of the author in 1897 at Trieste where he was the American Consul. The work stood still till 1816, when Deiters undertook to finish it; but he died in 1907 before he had published the second volume. Riemann finished the work from the materials left by Deiters. It is by far the most important work on Beethoven.

LUDWIG NOHL.—*Beethovens Leben*, 4 vols., 1864-1877.

LUDWIG NOHL.—*Beethoven nach den Schilder-ungen seiner Zeitgenossen*, Stuttgart.

A. B. MARZ.—*L. van Beethovens Leben und Schaffen*, 2 vols. 5th Edition revised by G. Behncke. Berlin, 1902.

VICTOR WILDER.—*Beethoven, sa vie et son œuvre*, 1883.

III.—FOR BEETHOVEN'S WORKS.

BEETHOVEN.—*Complete works*, critical edition, Breitkopf and Haertel, Leipzig, 38 vols.

G. NOTTEBOHM.—*Thematisches Verzeichniss der im Druck erschienen Werke von Ludwig van Beethoven*, Leipzig, 1868.

A. W. THAYER.—*Chronologisches Verzeichniss der Werke von Beethoven*. 1865.

G. NOTTEBOHM.—*Ein Skizzenbuch von Beethoven*. 1865.

G. NOTTEBOHM.—*Ein Skizzenbuch von Beethoven. aus dem Jahre*, 1803. 1880.

G. NOTTEBOHM.—*Beethovens Studien*. 1873.

G. NOTTEBOHM.—*Beethoveniana. Zweite Beethoveniana*. 1872-87.

GEORGE GROVE.—*Beethoven and his Nine Symphonies*. London, Novello, 1896.

J. G. PRODHOMME.—*Les Symphonies de Beethoven*, 1906.

ALFREDO COLOMBANI.—*Le Nove Sinfonie di Beethoven*. Turin, 1897.

ERNST VON ELTERLEIN.—*Beethovens Claviersonaten*. Fifth edition, 1895.

WILLIBALD NAGEL.—*Beethoven und seine Klaviersonaten*. Two volumes, 1903-1905.

J. S. SHEDLOCK.—*The Pianoforte Sonata*. London, Methuen, 1900.

CHARLES CZERNY.—*Pianoforte School* (part 4, chapters 2 and 3).

THEODOR HELM.—*Beethoven's Streichquartette.* 1885.

H. DE CURZON.—*Les lieder et airs detaches de Beethoven,* 1906.

OTTO JAHN.—*Leonore. Klavierauszug mit Text, nach der zweiten Bearbeitung,* 1852.

DR. ERICH PRIEGER.—*Fidelio. Klavierauszug mit Text, nach der ersten Bearbeitung,* 1906.

WILHELM WEBER.—*Beethovens Missa Solemnis,* 1897.

MARIAN TENGER.—*Beethoven s Unsterbliche Geliebte,* 1890. The historical value of this book has been frequently contested. Marian Tenger was the confidential friend of Theresa in her last years. It is very likely that Theresa, then aged, may involuntarily have idealised her remembrances; but the foundation of the story appears reliable.

A. EHRHARD.—*Franz Grillparzer,* 1900.

THEODOR VON FRIMMEL.—*Ludwig van Beethoven* (in the collection of *Berühmte, Musiker*), Berlin, 1901.

JEAN CHANTAVOINE.—*Beethoven,* Paris, 1907.

DR. ALFRED CHRISTIAN KALISCHER.—*Beethoven und seiner Zeitgenossen Beitrage zur Geschichte des Kunstlers und Menschen.* 4 vols., 1910. A collection of documents of the greatest interest on the whole circle of

Beethoven's friends. This wealth of information renews in a great part the psychology of Beethoven.

PROF. DR. RICHARD STERNFELD.—*Zur Einfuhrung in Ludwig von Beethoven's Missa Solemnis.*

IGNAZ VON SEYFRIED.—*Ludwig von Beethoven im Generalbass, Kontrapunkt, und in der Kompositions Lehre,* 1832.

W. DE LENZ.—*Beethoven et ses trois styles.* (Analysis of his pianoforte sonatas), (out of print), 1854.

OULIBICHEFF.—*Beethoven, ses critiques et ses glossateurs,* 1857.

WASIELEWSKI.—*Beethoven,* 2 volumes, Berlin, 1886.

R. SCHUMANN.—*Music and Musicians.* Translated by Fanny Raymond Ritter, London, Reeves.

RICHARD WAGNER.—*Beethoven.* Leipzig, 1870

VINCENT D'INDY.—*Beethoven.* Paris, 1911.

• • • • • •

BEETHOVEN'S PORTRAITS.

1789.—*Silhouette of Beethoven at eighteen years.*
(Beethoven's house at Bonn; reproduced in
Frimmel's Biography, page 16).

1791-2.—*Miniature of Beethoven* by Gerhard von
Kügelgen. (In the possession of George Hens-
chel, London; reproduced in "Musical
Times" of December, 1892, page 8).

1801.—*Drawing by G. Stainhauser,* engraved by
Johann Neidl. (Reproduced in " Les Musi-
ciens," celebres by Felix Clement, 1878, page
267; Frimmel, page 28).

1802.—*Engraving by Scheffner,* after Stainhauser.
(Beethoven's house at Bonn; reproduced in
"Die Musik," of March 15th, 1902, page
1145).

1802.—*Miniature of Beethoven,* by Christian
Hornemann. (In the possession of Madame
de Breuning at Vienna; reproduced in
Frimmel, page 31).

1805.—*Portrait of Beethoven* by W. J. Mahler.
(In the possession of Robert Heimler, Vienna;
reproduced in "Musical Times," December,
1892, page 7; " Frimmel," page 34).

1808.—*Drawing by L. F. Schnorr de Carolsfeld,*
lithographed by J. Bauer. (Beethoven's house
at Bonn).

1812.—*Cast of Beethoven,* modelled by Franz Klein.

1812.—*Bust of Beethoven,* by Franz Klein, from the cast. (Belonging to E. Streicher, piano manufacturer, in Vienna; reproduced in Frimmel, page 46; " Musical Times," December, 1892, page 19).

1814.—*Drawing by L. Letronne,* engraved by Blasius Hoefel. (The finest portrait of Beethoven; Beethoven's house at Bonn contains the original, which he offered to Wegeler; reproduced in Frimmel, page 51; " Musical Times," December, 1892, page 21).

1815.—*Drawing by L. Letronne,* engraved by Riedel. (Reproduced in " Die Musik," page 1147).

1815.—*Second portrait of Beethoven,* by Mahler. (In the possession of Ignace von Gleichenstein of Fribourg-en-Brisgau. Reproduction in Beethoven's house at Bonn).

1815.—*Portrait of Beethoven, by Christian Heckel.* (In the possession of J. F. Heckel, of Mannheim; reproduction in Beethoven's house at Bonn).

1818.—*Engraving* from the drawing of Beethoven by Aug. von Kloeber. (Reproduced in " Musical Times," December, 1892, page 25). The original drawing by Kloeber is in the collection of Dr. Erich Prieger at Bonn.

1819.—*Portrait of Beethoven* by K. Joseph Stieler.

(The property of Alex. Meyer Cohn, Berlin; reproduced in Frimmel, page 71).

1821.—*Bust of Beethoven* by Anton Dietrich. (In the possession of Leopold Schrotter, of Kristelli; reproduction in Beethoven's house at Bonn).

1824-6.—*Caricatures of Beethoven walking*, by J. P. Lyser. (Original in the Gesellschaft der Musikfreunde, Vienna; reproduced in Frimmel, page 67; "Musical Times," December, 1892, page 15).

1823.—*Caricatures of Beethoven walking*, by Jos. van Boehm. (Reproduced in Frimmel, page 70).

1823.—*Portrait of Beethoven* by Waldmueller. (Belonging to Messrs. Breitkopf and Haertel, Leipzig; reproduced in Frimmel, page 72).

1825-6.—*Drawing of Beethoven* by Stepan Decker. (In the possession of George Decker, Vienna; reproductions in Beethoven's house at Bonn).

1826.—*Drawing of Beethoven* by A. Dietrich, lithographed by Jos. Kriehuber. (Reproduced in Frimmel, page 73).

1826.—*Bust of Beethoven a la antique*, by Schaller. (The property of the Philharmonic Society of London; copy in Beethoven's house at Bonn; reproduced in Frimmel, page 74, and in "Musical Times," December, 1892).

1827.—*Sketch of Beethoven on his death-bed*, by

Jos. Danhauser. (In the possession A. Artaria, Vienna; reproduced in the " Allgemeine Musik-Zeitung " of April 19th, 1901.

1827.—*Three sketches of Beethoven on his deathbed*, by Teltscher. (In the possession of Dr. Aug. Heymann; published by Frimmel; reproduced in the " Courier Musical " of November 15th, 1909).

1827.—*Mask of Beethoven dead*, modelled by Danhauser. (Beethoven's house at Bonn).

Numerous portraits of Beethoven have been made since his death. The most remarkable work which has been dedicated to his memory is the monument of Max Klinger (Vienna, 1902).

CLASSIFICATION OF
BEETHOVEN'S PIANOFORTE SONATAS
IN ORDER OF STUDY

CLASSIFICATION OF
BEETHOVEN'S PIANOFORTE SONATAS.
IN ORDER OF STUDY

1. Op. 49, No. 2, in G major.
2. Op. 49, No. 1, in G minor.
3. Op. 14, No. 2, in G major.
4. Op. 14, No. 1, in E major.
5. Op. 79, in G major.
6. Op. 2, No. 1, in F minor.
7. Op. 10, No. 1, in C minor.
8. Op. 10, No. 2, in F major.
9. Op. 10, No. 3, in D major.
10. Op. 13, in C minor (*Pathétique*).
11. Op. 22, in B flat major.
12. Op. 28, in D major (*Pastorale*).
13. Op. 2, No. 2, in A major.
14. Op. 2, No. 3, in C major.
15. Op. 7, in E flat major.
16. Op. 26, in A flat major.
17. Op. 31, No. 1, in G major.
18. Op. 31, No. 3, in E flat major.
19. Op. 90, in E minor.
20. Op. 54, in F major.

21. Op. 27, No. 1, in E flat major.
22. Op. 27, No. 2 in C sharp minor. (*Moon-light*).
23. Op. 31, No. 2 in D minor.
24. Op. 53, in C major.
25. Op. 81, in E flat major. (*Les Adieux*).
26. Op. 78, in F sharp major.
27. Op. 57, in F minor. (*Appassionata*).
28. Op. 110, in A flat major.
29. Op. 109, in E major.
30. Op. 101, in A major.
31. Op. 111, in C minor.
32. Op. 106, in B flat major. (*The Giant*).

COMPLETE LIST
OF BEETHOVEN'S COMPOSITIONS

LIST OF BEETHOVEN'S WORKS.

Compiled from Marx and Thayer.

I.—COMPOSITIONS WITH OPUS NUMBER

Opus

1. *Three Trios* for pianoforte, violin, and violoncello, in E flat, G major, and C minor; dedicated to Prince Lichnovsky; composed 1791-92.

2. *Three Sonatas* for piano, in F minor, A major, and C major; dedicated to Joseph Haydn; published 1796.

3. *Trio* for violin, viola, violoncello, in E flat; composed in Bonn before 1792.

4. *Quintet* for two violins, two violas, and violoncello, in E flat (from octet for wind instruments, Op. 103); published 1795.

5. *Two Sonatas* for piano and violoncello, in F major and G minor; dedicated to Frederic William II. of Prussia; composed in Berlin in 1796.

6. *Sonata* for piano, for four hands, in D major; published 1796-97.

7. *Sonata* for piano, in E flat; dedicated to

the Countess Babette von Keglevics;
published 1797.

8. *Serenade* for violin, viola, and violoncello,
in D major; published 1797.

9. *Three Trios* for violin, viola, and violoncello, in G major, D major, and C minor;
dedicated to the Count von Brovne;
published 1798.

10. *Three Sonatas* for piano, in C minor, F
major, and D major; dedicated to the
Countess von Brovne; published 1798.

11. *Trio* for piano, clarionet (or violin), and violoncello, in B flat; dedicated to the
Countess von Thun; published 1798.

12. *Three Sonatas* for piano and violin, in D
major, A major, and E flat major; dedicated to F. A. Salieri; published 1798-99.

13. *Sonata Pathétique* for piano, in C minor;
dedicated to Prince Lichnovsky; published
1799.

14. *Two Sonatas* for piano, in E major and G
major; dedicated to the Baroness Braun;
published 1799.

15. *First Concerto* for piano and orchestra, in
C major; dedicated to the Princess
Odescalchy, *née* Countess von Keglevics;
composed 1795.

16. *Quintet* for piano, clarionet, oboe, bassoon,
and horn, in E flat major; dedicated to
the Prince von Schwarzenberg; performed
1798.

17. *Sonata* for piano and horn, in F major; dedicated to the Baroness Braun; composed
1800.

18. *Six Quartets* for two violins, viola, and
violoncello, in F major, G major, D
major, C minor, A major, and B flat
major; dedicated to Prince Lobkovitz;
published 1800-1801.

19. *Second Concerto* for piano and orchestra, in
B flat major; dedicated to M. von Nickels-
berg; composed 1798.

20. *Grand Septet* for violin, viola, violoncello,
horn, clarionet, bassoon, and double-bass,
in E flat; performed 1800.

21. *First Symphony* for orchestra, in C major;
dedicated to the Baron van Swieten; performed 1800.

22. *Grand Sonata* for piano, in B flat; dedicated
to the Count von Browne; composed 1800.

23. *Sonata* for piano and violin, in A minor;
dedicated to Count Moritz von Fries;
published 1801.

24. *Sonata* for piano and violin, in F major;
dedicated to Count Moritz von Fries;
published 1801 (originally together with
Op. 23).

25. *Serenade* for flute, violin, and viola, in D
major; published 1802.

26. *Sonata* for piano, in A flat; dedicated to
Prince Lichnovsky; composed 1801.

27. *Two Sonatas quasi Fantasia,* for piano, No. 1, in E flat major, dedicated to the Princess Lichtenstein; No. 2, in C sharp minor, dedicated to the Countess Julia Guicciardi; composed 1801 (?).

28. *Sonata* for piano, in D major; dedicated to M. von Sonnenfels; composed 1801.

29. *Quintet* for two violins, two violas, and violoncello, in C major; dedicated to Count von Fries; composed 1801.

30. *Three Sonatas* for piano and violin, in A major, C minor, and G major; dedicated to the Emperor Alexander I. of Russia; composed 1802.

31. *Three Sonatas* for piano, in G major, D minor, & E flat major; composed 1802 (?).

32. *To Hope,* words from the *Urania* of Tiedge; published 1805 (first setting; see Op. 94).

33. *Bagatelles* for piano; composed 1782.

34. *Six Variations* for piano, in F major, or an original theme; dedicated to the Princess Odescalchy; composed in 1802 (?).

35. *Fifteen Variations with a Fugue,* for piano, on a theme from " Prometheus "; dedicated to Count Maritz Lichnovsky; composed 1802.

36. *Second Symphony* for orchestra, in D major; dedicated to Prince Lichnovsky; composed 1802.

37. *Third Concerto* for piano and orchestra, in

C minor; dedicated to Prince Louis Ferdinand of Prussia; composed 1800.

38. *Trio* for piano, clarionet (or violin), and violoncello (from the *Septet,* Op. 20), published 1805.

39. *Two Preludes through all the major and minor keys,* for piano or organ; composed 1789.

40. *Romance* for violin and orchestra, in G major; composed 1802 (?).

41. *Serenade* for piano and flute (or violin), in D major; from Opus 5. Published 1803.

42. *Notturno* for piano and violoncello, in D major (from Op. 8); published 1804.

43. *Ballet,* " The Men of Prometheus "; composed 1800.

44. *Fourteen Variations* for piano, violin, ana violoncello, on an original theme; composed 1802 (?).

45. *Three Marches* for piano, for four hands, in C major, E flat major, and D major; dedicated to the Princess Esterhazy; composed 1802 (1801 ?).

46. *Adelaïde,* words by Matthison; composed 1796.

47. *Sonata* for piano and violin, in A major; dedicated to the violinist, Rudolph Kreutzer; composed 1803.

48. *Six spiritual songs,* by Gellert; published 1803.

49. *Two easy Sonatas* for piano, in G minor and G major; composed 1802 (?).
50. *Romance* for violin and orchestra, in F major; composed in 1802 (?).
51. *Two Rondos* for piano; No. 1 in C major, published 1798 (?); No. 2 in G major, dedicated to the Countess Henriette von Lichnovsky; published 1802.
52. *Eight Songs;* words by Claudius, Sophie von Mereau, Burger, Goethe, and Lessing; partly composed in Bonn before 1792.
53. *Grand Sonata* for piano, in C major; dedicated to Count Waldstein; composed in 1803 (?).
54. *Sonata* for piano, in F major; composed 1803 (?).
55. *Third Symphony* (Eroica) for orchestra, in E flat; dedicated to Prince Lobkovitz; composed 1803-4.
56. *Triple Concerto* for piano, violin and violoncello, with orchestra, in C major; composed 1804-5.
57. *Grand Sonata* for piano and orchestra, in G major; dedicated to the Count von Brunswick; composed 1804.
58. *Fourth Concerto* for piano and orchestra, in G major; dedicated to the Archduke Rudolph; composed 1806 (?).
59. *Three Quartets* for two violins, viola, and violoncello, in F major, E minor, and C major; dedicated to Prince Rasumovsky; composed 1806.

60. *Fourth Symphony* for orchestra, in B flat; dedicated to Count Oppersdorf; composed 1806.

61. *Concerto* for violin and orchestra, in D major; dedicated to Stephan von Breuning; composed 1806.

62. *Overture, " Coriolanus,"* in C minor; dedicated to the dramatist, Heinrich von Collin; composed 1807.

63. *Sonata* for piano, violin, and violoncello (from the Octet, Op. 103); published 1807.

64. *Sonata* for piano, violin, and violoncello from the Trio, Op. 3); published 1807.

65. *Scena and Aria, " Ah, perfido! "* for soprano voice and orchestra; dedicated to the Countess Clari; composed 1796.

66. *Twelve Variations* for piano and violoncello, in F major, on the theme, *Ein Madchen oder Weibchen,* from Mozart's *Zauberflote;* published 1798.

67. *Fifth Symphony* for orchestra, in C minor; dedicated to Prince Lobkovitz and Count Rasumovsky; composed 1808 (?).

68. *Sixth Symphony (Pastoral)* for orchestra, in F major; dedicated to Prince Lobkovitz and Count Rasumovsky; composed 1808 (?).

69. *Sonata* for piano and violoncello, in A major; dedicated to Baron von Gleichenstein; published 1809.

70. *Two Trios* for piano, violin, and violoncello,
     in D major and E flat major; dedicated
     to the Countess Marie Erdödy; composed
     1808.

71   *Sextet* for two clarionets, two flutes, and two
     bassoons; performed 1804-5.

72. *Fidelio* (*Leonora*) opera in two acts; com-
     posed 1804-5.

73. *Fifth Concerto* for piano and orchestra in
     E flat; dedicated to the Archduke
     Rudolph; composed 1809.

74. *Quartet* (tenth) for two violins, viola, and
     violoncello, in E flat; dedicated to Prince
     Lobkovitz; composed 1809.

7⁵   *Six Songs;* words by Goethe and Reissig;
     dedicated to the Princess Kinsky; com-
     posed 1810.

76. *Variations* for piano, in D major, on an
     original (?) theme, afterwards employed
     as the *Turkish March* in the *Ruins of
     Athens;* dedicated to his friend, Aliva;
     published 1810.

77. *Fantasia* for piano, in G minor; dedicated
     to the Count von Brunswick; composed
     1809.

78. *Sonata* for piano, in F sharp major; dedi-
     cated to the Countess von Brunswick;
     composed 1809.

79. *Sonatina* for piano, in G major; published
     1810.

80. *Fantasia* for piano, orchestra, and chorus, in C minor; words, " Schmeichelnd hold und lieblich klingen," by Kuffner; dedicated to Joseph Maximilian, of Bavaria; performed 1808.

81A. *Sonata* for piano, *Les Adieux*, in E flat; dedicated to the Archduke Rudolph; composed 1809.

81B. *Sextet* for two violins, viola, violoncello, and two horns (*obbligato*) in E flat; published 1810.

82. *Four Ariettas and a Duet*, with pianoforte accompaniment; words of Nos. 2, 3, and 5, by Mestastasio; published 1811.

83. *Three Songs;* words by Goethe; dedicated to the Princess Kinsky; composed 1810.

84. *Overture and Incidental Music to " Egmont ";* composed 1809-10.

85. *" The Mount of Olives,"* an *oratorio;* text by Franz Xaver Huber; composed 1800 (?).

86. *First Mass* for four voices and orchestra, in C major; dedicated to Prince Esterhazy; composed 1807.

87. *Trio* for wind instruments, in C major; performed 1797.

88. *" Das Gluck der Freundschaft "* for voice and piano; published 1803.

89. *Polonaise* for piano, in C major; dedicated to the Empress Elisabeth Alexievna of Russia; composed 1814.

90. *Sonata* for piano, in E minor; dedicated to Count Moritz Lichnowski; composed 1814.

91. *The Battle of Vittoria* for orchestra; dedicated to the Prince Regent of England; composed 1813.

92. *Seventh Symphony* for orchestra, in A major; dedicated to Count Fries; composed 1812.

93. *Eighth Symphony* for orchestra, in F major: composed 1812.

94. " *To Hope,*" *words from the* " *Urania* " *of Tiegde* (second setting see Op. 32); composed 1816.

95. *Quartet* for two violins, viola, and violoncello, in F minor; dedicated to Secretary Zmeskall; composed 1810.

96. *Sonata* for piano and violin, in G major; dedicated to the Archduke Rudolph; composed 1810.

97. *Trio* for piano, violin, and violoncello, in B flat; dedicated to the Archduke Rudolph; composed 1811.

98. *An die ferne Geliebte,* (a *Liederkreis*); words by Jeitteles; dedicated to Prince Lobkovitz; composed 1816.

99. *Der Mann von Wort,* for voice and piano; words by Kleinschmid; published 1815.

100. *Merkenstein,* for one or two voices and piano; words by Rupprecht; composed 1814.

101. *Sonata* for piano, in A major; dedicated to
the Baroness Erdmann; composed 1815.

102. *Two Sonatas* for piano and violoncello, in C
major and D major; dedicated to the
Countess Erdödy; composed 1815.

103. *Octet* for wind instruments, in E flat major;
composed in Bonn before 1792.

104. *Quintet* for two violins, two violas, and
violoncello, in C minor (from the Trio,
No. 3, of Op. 1); published 1819.

105. *Six themes varied* for piano, with violin ad
libitum; composed for George Thomson,
Edinburgh, 1818-19.

106. *Sonata* for piano, in B flat; dedicated to
the Archduke Rudolph; composed 1818.

107. *Ten Themes variés russes, écossais, tyro-
lienne* for piano, with violin *ad libitum;*
composed for George Thomson, 1818-20.

108. *Twenty-five Scotch Melodies* for one or two
voices, and chorus (*obbligato*); published
1825.

109. *Sonata* for piano, in E major; dedicated to
Fräulein Brentano; composed 1821 (?).

110. *Sonata* for piano, in A flat major; composed
1821.

111. *Sonata* for piano, in C minor; dedicated to
the Archduke Rudolph; composed 1822.

112. *Meeresstille und glückliche Fahrt* for four
voices and orchestra; dedicated to " the
Author of the Poem, the immortal
Goethe," composed 1815.

113. *Overture, " The Ruins of Athens ";* composed 1811-12.

114. *Marches and Choruses from " The Ruins of Athens."*

115. *Overture, " Namensfeier,"* in C major; dedicated to Prince Radzivill; composed 1814.

116. *Terzetto* for soprano, tenor, and bass, with orchestral accompaniment; composed 1801.

117. *Overture and Choruses, " King Stephen ";* performed 1812.

118. *Elegy* in memory of the Baroness Pasqualati, " Sanft wie du lebtest hast du vollendet " dedicated to the Baron Pasqualati; composed 1814.

119. *Twelve Bagatelles* for piano; composed 1820-1822.

120. *Thirty-three Variations on a waltz by Diabelli;* dedicated to Madame Brentano; composed 1823.

121A. *Adagio, Variations and Rondo* for piano, violin, and violoncello, in G major; theme, " Ich bin der Schneider Kakadu "; published 1824.

121B. *Opferlied* for solo, chorus, and orchestra; words by Matthison; composed 1822.

122. *In allen guten Stunden,* for solo and chorus, with two clarionets, two horns, and two bassoons; words by Goethe; composed 1822.

123. *Missa Solemnis* for four voices, chorus, and orchestra, in D major; dedicated to the Cardinal Archduke Rudolph; composed 1818-1822.

124. *Overture, " Weihe des Hauses,"* in C major; dedicated to Prince Galitzin; composed 1822.

125. *Ninth Symphony* with final chorus on Schiller's *" Ode to Joy"* for orchestra, four voices, and chorus, in D minor; dedicated to Frederick William III of Prussia; composed 1822-3.

126. *Six Bagatelles* for piano; composed about 1821.

127. *Quartet* for two violins, viola, and violoncello, in E flat; dedicated to Prince Galitzin; composed 1824.

128. *" The Kiss," Arietta* for voice and piano; composed 1822.

129. *Rondo capriccioso,* in G major.

130. *Quartet* for two violins, viola, and violoncello, in B flat; dedicated to Prince Galitzin; composed 1825.

131. *Quartet* for two violins, viola, and violoncello, in C sharp minor; dedicated to the Baron von Stutterheim; composed 1826.

132. *Quartet* for two violins, viola, and violoncello, in A minor; dedicated to Prince Galitzin; composed 1825.

133. *Grand Fugue* for two violins, viola, and

Q

- violoncello, in B flat; dedicated to the Cardinal Archduke Rudolph; composed 1825.

134. *Grand Fugue,* Op. 133 (arranged for piano for four hands).

135. *Quartet* (the sixteenth) for two violins, viola, and cello, in F major; dedicated to Herrn Wolfmeier; composed 1826.

136. *Der Glorreiche Augenblick,* cantata for four voices and orchestra; text by Dr. Weissenbach; dedicated to Franz I Emperor of Austria, Nicholas I Emperor of Russia, and Frederick William III King of Prussia; composed 1814.

137. *Fugue* for two violins, two violas, and cello, in D major; composed 1817.

138. *Ouverture caracteristique,* " *Leonora,*" No. 1, in C major.

II.—COMPOSITIONS DESIGNATED SIMPLY BY NUMBERS.

1A. *Twelve Variations* for piano and violin, in F major; Theme, *Se vuol ballare,* from Mozart's *Figaro;* dedicated to Eleanore von Breuning; published 1793. (See page 70).

1B. *Thirteen Variations* for piano, in A major; Theme, *Es war einmal ein alter Mann;* published 1794.

2. *Nine Variations* for piano in A major; Theme, *Quant è più bello;* published 1797.

3A. *Six Variations* for piano; Theme, *Nel cor più non mi sento;* composed 1795.

3B. *Two Minuets* for piano, for four hands.

4. *Twelve Variations* for piano, in C major; Theme, *Menuet à la Vigano;* published 1796.

5A. *Twelve Variations* for piano, in A major; Theme from the ballet of the *Wood maiden;* published 1797.

5B. *Twelve Variations* for piano and violoncello, in G major; Theme, " See, the Conquering Hero comes! " published 1804.

6. *Twelve Variations* for piano and violoncello, in F major (see Op. 66).

7. *Eight Variations* for piano, in C major; Theme from Grétry's *Richard Cœur de Lion;* published 1798.

8. *Ten Variations* for piano, in B flat major; Theme, *La stessa, la stessissima;* published 1799.

9. *Seven Variations* for piano, in F major; Theme, *Kind willst du ruhig schlafen;* published 1799.

10A. *Eight Variations* for piano, in F major; Theme, *Tändeln and Scherzen;* composed 1799.

10B. *Seven Variations* for piano and violoncello, in E flat; Theme from *The Magic Flute;* composed 1801 (?).

11. *Six very easy Variations on an original Theme;* composed 1801.

12. *Six easy Variations* for piano or harp, in F major; Theme, Swiss Air; published 1799 (?).

13. *Twenty-four Variations* for piano, in D major, on a Theme by Righini; composed about 1790.

14-23. Missing.

24. *Der Wachtelschlag* for voice and piano; words by Sauter; published 1804.

25. *Seven Variations* for piano, in C major; Theme, *God save the King;* published 1804.

26. *Five Variations* (favourite) for piano, in D major; Theme, *Rule Britannia;* published 1804.

27. *Six Variations* for piano, for four hands, in D major, on an original Theme; composed 1800.

28. *Minuet* for piano.

29. *Prelude* for piano, in F minor; published 1805.

30-31. Missing.

32. *To Hope* by Tiedge (see Op. 94).

33-34. Missing.

35. *Andante* for piano in F major (originally in the Sonata, Op. 53); composed 1803 (?).
36. *Thirty-two Variations* for piano, in C minor, on an original Theme; published 1807.
37. Missing.
38. *Die Sehnsucht* four melodies for voice and piano; text by Goethe; published 1810.

III.—COMPOSITIONS DESIGNATED BY LETTERS.

A.—INSTRUMENTAL MUSIC.

(a) *Trio* for piano, violin, and violoncello (in one movement), in B flat; dedicated to " My little friend, Maximiliana Brentano, for her encouragement in pianoforte playing "; composed 1812.

(b) *Rondo* for piano and violin, in G major; published 1800.

(c) *Andante* for piano, in G.

(d) *Sonata* for piano, in C major (incomplete); composed 1796.

(e) *Two easy Sonatinas* for piano, in G major and F major; composed in Bonn.

(f) *Three Sonatas* for piano, in E flat major, F minor, and D major; dedicated to the Elector, Max. Friedrich; composed at the age of ten.

(g) *Rondo* for piano, in A major; published 1784.

(h) *Andante* on the text, " Oh Hoffnung, du stählst die Herzen." (Ex. for the Archduke Rudolph).

(i) *Favourite March* of the Emperor Alexander.

(k) *Eight Variations* for piano, in B flat; Theme, *Ich habe ein kleines Hüttchen nur*.

(l) *Variations* for piano, on a March by Dressler; composed at the age of ten.

(m) *Variations* for piano, for four hands, on an original theme.

(n) *Variations* for piano, for four hands, in A major.

(o) *Triumphal March* for orchestra, in C major; performed 1813.

(p) *Second and Third Overtures to " Leonora "* (" Fidelio "), in C major.

(q) *Overture to " Fidelio "* (" Leonora," No. 4), in E flat.

(r) *Triumphal March* for orchestra in G major.

(s) *Three Duos* for clarionet and bassoon, in C major, F major, and B flat; composed about 1800.

(t) *Minuet* for piano (from the Septet, Op. 20).

(u) *Quintet* (MS.), for two violins, two violas, and violoncello in F major.

B.—DANCE MUSIC.

Twelve Contre-danses.
Twelve Minuets for orchestra.
Six Minuets for piano.
Twelve Danses Allemandes for two violins and bass.
Seven Country Dances for piano.
Six Country dances for piano.
Twelve Ecossaises for piano.
Six Allemandes for piano and violin.
Twelve Waltzes with Trios for orchestra.
Six Waltzes for two violins and bass.
Two Minuets for piano, for four hands.
Six Country Dances for piano.
Two favourite Waltzes for piano, in B flat major and F minor.

C.—VOCAL MUSIC.

a. *Six Songs* from Reissig's " *Blümchen der Einsamkeit* " :—

    1. *Sehnsucht,* in E major.

    2. *Krieger's Abschied,* in E flat.

    3. *Der Jüngling in der Fremde,* in B flat.

4. *An den fernen Geliebten,* in **G** major.
5. *Der Zufriedene,* in A major.
6. *Der Liebende,* in D major.

b. *Three Songs* :—

1. *An die Geliebte,* in B flat.
2. *Das Geheimniss,* in G major.
3. *So oder so! Nord oder Süd.*

c. *Italian and German Songs* :—

1. *La Partenza* (" ecco quel fiore ").
2. *Trinklied.*
3. *Liedchen von der Ruhe.*
4. *An die Hoffnung.*
5. *Ich liebe dich, so wie du nich.*
6. *Molly's Abschied.*
7. *Ohne Liebe.*
8. *Wachtelgesang.*
9. *Marmotte.*
10. *Maigesang.*
11. *Feuerfarbe.*
12. *Ecco quel fiori istanti.*

d. *Songs* for one or more voices, from Shakespeare, Byron, and Moore.

e. *Der Glorreiche Augenblick* for four voices and orchestra.

f. *Lied aus der Ferne.*

g.   *Three Songs* from Tiedge.

h.   *Three Songs*.

i.   *Three Songs*.

k.   *Oh! dass ich dir vom stillen Auge.*

l.   *Sehnsucht nach dem Rhein.*

m.   *Die Klage.*

n.   *Three Andantes.*

o.   *Ruf vom Berge.*

p.   *Der Bardengeist.*

q.   *Als die Geliebte sich trennen wollte.*

r.   *Elegy* on the death of a Poodle.

s.   *Arietta* in A flat major.

t.   *Canon* in E flat major.

u.   *Zärtliche Liebe.*

v.   *Resignation,* and *Lisch' aus,* in E major.

w.   *Canon* for six voices.

x.   *Canon* for four voices.

y.   *Canon* for three voices.

z.   *Canon* written in the album of Director
     Neide.

tz.   *Song of the Monks,* from Schiller's *William
     Tell.*

a2.   *Song of the Nightingale.*

b2.   *Germania's Wiedergeburt* for four voices
     and orchestra.

c2.   *Abschiedsgesang an Wiens Bürger.*

e2.   *Final Songs* from (1) *Die Ehrenpforte,* in
     D major; (2) *Die gute Nachricht.*

Q*

f2.   *Andenken von Matthison*—allegretto.

g.   *Three-part Song.*

- - -

IV.—COMPOSITIONS WHICH APPEARED AFTER BEETHOVEN'S DEATH, WITHOUT BEING DESIGNATED AS OPUS OR NUMBER.

a.   *Beethoven's Heimgang* for voice and piano.

b.   *An Sie*, Song, in A flat major.

c.   *Two Songs* :—
   1. *Seufzer eines Ungeliebten.*
   2. *Die laute Klage.*

d.   *Die Ehre Gottes in der Natur* for four voices and orchestra, in C major.

e.   *Cantata, " Europa steht."*

f.   *Song, " Gedenke mein."*

g.   *Empfindungen bei Lydia's Untreu,* in E flat.

h.   *Equali,* two pieces for four trombones.

i.   *Allegretto* for orchestra.

k.   *Three Quartets.*

l.   *Rondo* for piano and orchestra.

m. *Octet* for wind instruments.
n. *Rondino* for eight-part harmony.
o. *Two Trios* for piano, violin and Violoncello.
p. *Military March* for piano.
q. *Lament at Beethoven's Grave.*
r. *The Last Musical Thought.*

INDEX

INDEX

239